We know the exact time of Mozart's death: four
minutes to one o'clock in the morning of December
5th, 1791. From then on there are many questions.

At three o'clock the following afternoon, the brief
funeral service was held, not in the main body of
St. Stephen's Cathedral, but in a small vestibule.
The public was not informed in advance.
Constanze was not present at the service or the
burial, where it is believed that the body of
Mozart was quietly lowered into an unmarked
communal grave...

MOZART & CONSTANZE

FRANCIS CARR

 A DISCUS BOOK/PUBLISHED BY AVON BOOKS

AVON BOOKS
A division of
The Hearst Corporation
1790 Broadway
New York, New York 10019

Copyright © 1983 by Francis Carr
Published by arrangement with Franklin Watts, Inc.
Library of Congress Catalog Card Number: 84-091258
ISBN: 0-380-69884-6

First Discus Printing, May 1985

DISCUS TRADEMARK REG. U.S. PAT. OFF. AND IN
OTHER COUNTRIES, MARCA REGISTRADA, HECHO EN
U.S.A.

Printed in the U.S.A.

OPB   10 9 8 7 6 5 4 3 2 1

Contents

To Brigid Brophy,

a great Mozartian

Introduction

THE WIFE of a genius is often misjudged. Mozart's wife, Constanze, is no exception. But while some of her failings have been noted, there has been little examination of her true feelings while he was alive, at the time of his death and during her long widowhood.

Little is known of her before their marriage. In contrast, Mozart had been a celebrated pianist and composer for twenty years, having played in the capitals of Europe since the age of six. Constanze was marrying a famous man, whose life can be documented in detail. He was blessed from the start with a splendid string of names: Johann Chrysostom Wolfgang Theophilus Mozart.* No other composer before or since has been charged with such intense drive, with such early and seemingly effortless mastery. Even Beethoven must have envied Mozart's sublime skill in internal composition. Mozart's rapidly written scores are masterpieces of neatness and clarity while those of Beethoven are often pock-marked with alterations, deletions and repeated revisions of particular passages. Proof of the speed of Mozart's composition lies in his immense output in the last fifteen years of his life.

Born in the beautiful town of Salzburg on January 27th 1756, his life, from the start, was based upon a Court, that of the Prince Archbishop of Salzburg, a state enjoying its last decades of independence. Leopold Mozart, Wolfgang's father, was the Court violin-master, the author of a treatise on violin-playing, which soon became a standard work on the subject in the German-speaking world, and a composer. His mother, Anna

* Instead of Theophilus, his father translated the word into the German Gottlieb and in Latin, Amadeus, the name by which he came to be known.

Maria Pertl, was the daughter of another Court official. When he was only three, Mozart would sit beside his talented elder sister, Maria Anna, and watch her playing the clavier. A minuet and trio 'were learned by Wolfgangerl,' his father tells us, 'in half an hour, at half-past nine at night, on January 26th 1761, one day before his fifth birthday.'

In the following year, Leopold determined to travel with his two talented children, taking them first to Munich then to Vienna. News of their success in Munich and Linz preceded them to Vienna and as soon as the Empress Maria Theresa knew of their arrival in the capital, 'the command came for us to go to court'. At the Imperial summer palace of Schönbrunn, just outside the town, 'Their Majesties [the Empress and her husband Francis I] received us with extraordinary graciousness. Wolferl jumped up on the Empress's lap, put his arms round her neck and kissed her heartily. We were there from three to six o'clock.' Maria Theresa's daughter, Marie-Antoinette the future Queen of France, was there, aged seven. Mozart was greatly taken with her; when he tumbled on the polished floor, Marie-Antoinette picked him up. Mozart thanked her and said, 'You are good. I will marry you.'

Such was the success of this tour that Leopold was encouraged to embark on a more extended progress – to Mannheim, Frankfurt, Brussels, Paris and London. In Brussels, at the age of seven and a half, Wolfgang composed his first sonata. This, together with three more sonatas, was published in Paris when the Mozart family arrived in the capital. King Louis XV and his queen now received Wolfgang, his parents and his sister at Versailles. A special reception or *grand couvert* was held there on New Year's Eve and Madame de Pompadour was present.

In a long letter to a friend in Salzburg (dated February 1st 1764), Leopold Mozart described this great occasion:

It is not the custom here to kiss the hand of royal persons, or to disturb them with a petition, or even to speak to them *au passage* ... Hence you can well imagine how impressed and amazed these French people must have been when the King's daughters in the public gallery stopped when they saw my children, came up to them and not only allowed them to kiss their hands, but kissed them innumerable times. And the same thing happened with Madame la Dauphine [Maria Josepha, the mother of Louis XVI]. At the banquet on the evening of New Year's Day, not only was it necessary to make room for us all to go up to the royal table, but my Wolfgang was graciously privileged to stand beside the Queen the whole time, to talk constantly to her, entertain her and kiss her hands, besides partaking of the dishes which she handed him from the table.

You must know that the King never dines in public, except on Sunday evenings when the whole Royal Family dine together. But not everyone is allowed to be present. When there is a great festival, such as New Year's Day or Easter, the *grand couvert* is held, to which all persons of distinction are admitted. There is not, however, very much room and consequently the hall soon gets filled up. We arrived late. So the Swiss Guards had to make way for us and we were led through the hall into the room close to the royal table, through which the royal family enter. As the King and Queen passed us, they spoke to our Wolfgang, and we then followed them to the table.

The Queen [Maria Leczinska, daughter of the exiled King of Poland] speaks as good German as we do, and, as the King knows none, she interpreted to him everything that our gallant Wolfgang said. I stood beside him, and on the other side of the King stood my wife and daughter.

After five months in Paris they moved to London where Leopold and his children were initially even more successful. They stayed there for more than a year, from April 1764 to September the following year. Five days after their arrival, they were received at Court. Leopold has provided a lively picture of their welcome at Buckingham House (May 28th 1764).

The graciousness with which both his Majesty the King [George III] and Her Majesty the Queen received us cannot be described. In short, their easy manner and friendly ways made us forget that they were the King and Queen of England. At all courts up to the present we have been received with extraordinary courtesy. But the welcome which we have been given here exceeds all others. A week later we were walking in St James's Park. The King came along driving with the Queen and, although we all had on different clothes, they recognised us nevertheless and not only greeted us, but the King opened the window, leaned out and saluted us and especially our Master Wolfgang, nodding and waving his hand.

On May 19 we were again with the King and Queen, from six until ten in the evening, when the only other people present were the two princes, who are the King's brothers, and another, the brother of the Queen. The King placed before Wolfgang the works of J. C. Bach, Abel and Handel. He played so splendidly on the King's organ that they all value his organ-playing more highly than his clavier-playing. Then he accompanied the Queen in an aria which she sang, and also a flautist who played a solo. Finally he took the bass part of some airs of Handel (which happened to be lying there) and played the most beautiful melody on it and in such a manner that everybody was amazed. In short, what he knew when we left Salzburg is a mere shadow compared with what he knows now. It exceeds all that one can imagine.

In the *Public Advertiser*, on June 5th 1764, there appeared this announcement:

At the Great Room in Spring Garden, near St. James's Park, this day, at 12 o'clock, will be performed a Grand Concert of Vocal and Instrumental Music, for the benefit of Miss Mozart of eleven, and Master Mozart of eight years of age, Prodigies of Nature. Tickets, at half a guinea, to be had of Mr. Mozart, at Mr. Couzin's, Hair Cutter, in Cecil Court, St. Martin's Lane.

The Mozart family were staying at the address given. In August Leopold suffered a severe inflammation of the throat, and he was advised to move outside London to Chelsea, then a village, where, as he wrote, he 'could get some appetite and fresh strength from the good air. It has one of the most beautiful views in the world. Wherever I turn my eyes, I only see gardens and in the distance fine castles. The house in which

I live has a lovely garden.' This house still stands, no. 180/182 Ebury Street. Here the Mozarts stayed for seven weeks. Wolfgang was asked not to play the piano when they arrived, so as not to disturb his father. So he quietly composed. He wrote forty-three short pieces for the piano in a little music book his father had given him and these clearly show his genius emerging. For a long time nothing was known of this note book; in 1898 it was discovered in a private collection of manuscripts and presented to the Royal Library in Berlin. In addition to these compositions, he wrote, while in England, six sonatas for violin, one aria, a short choral composition, a piano duet and his first symphony, for strings, two oboes and four horns.

Wolfgang and his sister performed on many occasions at Ranelagh and Vauxhall, at the Swan and Hoop in Cornhill and at private houses. When the family returned to London in September 1765, they lived in Soho, at 21 Frith Street. In November Mozart was given 50 guineas by Queen Charlotte.

While Wolfgang was in London, he met Johann Christian Bach who, before coming to England had been organist of Milan Cathedral. He was the eighteenth child and eleventh son of Johann Sebastian and for the last twenty-five years of his life lived in London, as a composer, opera and concert director and music master of George III's family. He was known here and on the continent as 'the English Bach'. At one recital Bach and Mozart alternated as soloists in the same sonata so perfectly that no break in excellence could be detected. Mozart learnt much from Johann Christian; this friendship gave the young maestro his first contact with the elegance and refinement of the Italian style, an important element in J. C. Bach's compositions.

Three of Mozart's most important journeys were to Italy, between 1770 and 1773. Here he could absorb the music of Boccherini, Cimarosa, Alessandro and Domenico Scarlatti, Vivaldi and Pergolese. In Rome Pope Clement XIV conferred on Wolfgang the gold cross of the Order of the Golden Spur; the fourteen-year-old composer was now Sir Wolfgang, Signor Cavaliere Mozart. Writing to his wife, Leopold Mozart pointed out that 'it is the same order as Gluck's'. In the capital Wolfgang copied from memory Gregorio Allegri's *Miserere*, a beautiful work performed only during Holy Week, and seldom copied officially.

As in Paris and London, Wolfgang was welcomed by the highest in the land.

On 12th April [wrote his father], we were present at the cere-mony of the *Functiones*. We were standing beside the Pope at the top of the table. This was all the more amazing as we had to pass through two doors guarded by Swiss guards in armour, and make our way through hundreds of people. They took Wolfgang for some German courtier, while some even thought he was a prince. Thus we made our way to the Cardinals' table.

In Italy Mozart met Charles Edward, the young Pretender, who lived in Rome as Count of Albany, Sir William Hamilton, who had been Ambassador to the Court of Naples since 1764, his wife, the first Lady Hamilton, who, Mozart wrote, 'plays the clavier with unusual feeling', and Thomas Linley, who, at the same age as Wolfgang, had already become well-known in Italy as a violinist. Dr Burney, the musicologist, wrote that he was greatly admired in Florence, where he had been studying for two years. 'The *Tommasino*, as he is called, and the little Mozart are talked of all over Italy as the most promising geniuses of this age.' When he returned to England Linley became leader and soloist at his father's concerts in Bath, and composed sacred music. He was drowned at the age of twenty-two.

Mozart continued to compose with amazing rapidity and skill. Two comic operas, *La Finta Semplice* (*The Sham Simpleton*) and *Bastien und Bastienne*, were written at the age of twelve, and were followed by his first masses, an inspired stream of serenades, divertimenti and sonatas. At the age of eighteen, his opera, *La Finta Giardiniera* (*The Sham Gardener*) was an instant success. From Munich, where it was given its first performance, Mozart wrote:

Thank God! My opera was performed yesterday [January 13th 1775] and was such a success that it is impossible for me to describe the applause.

In the first place, the whole theatre was so packed that a great many people were turned away. Then after each aria there was a terrific noise, clapping of hands and cries of 'Viva Maestro'. Her Highness the Electress and the Dowager Electress (who were sitting opposite me) also called out 'Bravo'. Afterwards I went off with Papa to the room through which the Elector and the whole court had to pass and I kissed the hands of the Elector and Electress and Their Highnesses, who were all very gracious. Early this morning His Grace the Bishop of Chiemsee [Count Ferdinand von Zeill] sent me a message, congratulating me on the extraordinary success of my opera.

Mozart's letters give us an excellent insight into his humorous and playful character. There are surprises of one kind or another in every letter. From Bologna, when he was fourteen, he ended a letter to his sister with these words:

Addio! Farewell. My sole amusement at the moment consists in dancing English steps and in pirouetting and cutting capers. Italy is a sleepy country! I am always drowsy! Addio! Farewell.   [August 4th 1770]

In another letter to his sister the following year, written when he was in Milan, he described his apartment:

Upstairs we have a violinist, downstairs another one; in the next room a singing-master who gives lessons, and in the other room opposite ours an oboist. That is good fun when you are composing! It gives you plenty of ideas.   [August 24th 1771]

Mozart wrote a brief note to his sister from Vienna, when he was seventeen, which amusingly expresses his cosmopolitan mind.

Hodie nous avons begegnet per strada Dominum Edelbach, welcher uns di voi compliments ausgerichtet hat, et qui sich tibi et ta mère empfehlen lässt. Addio.   [August 12th 1773]

[Today in the street we met Mister Edelbach, who was given by us your compliments, and who sends you and your mother his best wishes.]

After writing a long letter to his father dated October 3rd 1777, when he and his mother were in Munich, he brought it to a close with this masterly re-ordering of syntax, graphically conveying fatigue and contentment.

I wish you a very restful night, and I improve on this good wish by hearing to hope soon that Papa is well quite. I forgiveness your crave for my disgraceful handwriting, but ink, haste, sleep, dreams and all the rest ... I Papa your, my hands kiss, a thousand times dearest, and my embrace, the heart, sister I with all my brute of a, and remain, now and for ever, amen,

> Wolfgang, most obedient your
> Amadé Mozart son

Mozart and his mother spent four months in Mannheim when he was twenty-one. He would have travelled with his father, but Archbishop Colloredo wanted Leopold to stay in Salzburg; on August 28th 1777, the Archbishop declared that 'father and son have my permission to seek their fortune elsewhere'; but a month later Leopold was informed that 'His Grace retains the petitioner in his employment and graciously commands him to endeavour to render good service both to the Church and to His Grace's person.'* Leopold described this note as a 'rigmarole of nonsense', but acquiesced. Mannheim had for many years been an important musical capital in Europe, thanks to its excellent orchestra and the encouragement of its ruler, Prince Karl Theodor.

For a fortnight Wolfgang and his mother Anna Maria stayed in Augsburg. Here he met his cousin, Maria Anna Thekla (Victoria), who made a great impression on him. He found her 'beautiful, intelligent, charming, clever and gay. We get on extremely well, for, like myself, she is a bit of a scamp. We

---

* *The Letters of Mozart and His Family*, arranged and translated by Emily Anderson. (Macmillan, 1938) Vol. 1, pp. 389, 408.

both laugh at everyone and have great fun.' They were fond of exchanging jokes, puns and general verbal tomfoolery and some of his most amusing letters were later written to her.

One of these letters, written from Mannheim on November 13th 1777, begins exultantly,

Ma très chère niece! cousine! fille! mère, soeur, et épouse!
Bless my soul, a thousand curses, Croatians, damnations, devils, witches, sorcerers, hell's battalions to all eternity, by all the elements, air, water, earth, and fire, Europe, Asia, Africa and America, Jesuits, Augustinians, Benedictines, Capuchins, Minorites, Franciscans, Dominicans, Carthusians and Brothers of the Holy Cross, Canons regular and irregular, all slackers, knaves, cowards, sluggards and toadies higgledy-piggledy, asses, buffaloes, oxen, fools, nit-wits and dunces! Such a parcel to get, but no portrait! ... Do go on loving me, as I love you ...
Je vous baise vos mains, votre visage, vos genoux, et votre – , enfin, tout ce que vous me permettez de baiser.

In another long letter (February 28th 1778), Mozart asked his cousin whether she was well.

Now I have the honour to enquire how you are and whether you perspire? Whether your stomach is still in good order? Whether indeed you have no disorder? Whether you still can like me at all? Whether with chalk you often scrawl? Whether now and then you have me in mind? Whether to hang yourself you sometimes feel inclined? Whether you have been wild? With this poor foolish child? Whether to make peace with me you'll be so kind? Ah, you're laughing! Victoria! Our arses shall be the symbol of our peacemaking! Why, of course, I'm sure of success, even if to-day I should make a mess, though to Paris I go in a fortnight or less.

Treating the language as freely as a composer handles a melody, a sequence of notes which can easily be played in reverse order, Mozart concluded another letter, dated November 5th 1777, to his sister in this manner:

Well, farewell. I kiss you 1000 times and remain, as always, your little old piggy wiggy

> Wolfgang Amadé Rosy Posy

A thousand compliments from us two travellers to my aunt and uncle. My greetings bleatings to all my good friends sends. Addio, booby looby.

> 333 to the grave, if my life I save
> Miehnnam, Rebotco eht 5,7771.

Mozart's attempts to secure employment at the Court of Prince Karl Theodor met with no definite response, although his compositions and he himself were valued highly by the aristocracy and the other friends he made in Mannheim. 'You cannot imagine in what high favour Wolfgang is here,' wrote his mother to Leopold, 'both with the orchestra and with other people. They all say that there is no one to touch him. They absolutely idolise his compositions.'

It was not only orchestral music that was beautifully played by the Prince's musicians. The first operas in German were here being planned and performed. In 1777 *Gunther von Schwarzburg* was produced in Mannheim; the composer was Ignaz Holzbauer, the *Kapellmeister*. The stage was set in the German-speaking world for a national opera. This could be the opportunity for Mozart to establish himself as the court composer.

I

The Abduction
1778–81

I'm an English woman, born to liberty. I will defy anyone who tries to force me to do anything! Such an ugly old creature should not dare to give orders to a girl like me, young, beautiful and free, as if I were a kitchen maid. I am the mistress here!

Blonde to Osmin, in BELMONTE UND CONSTANZE *or* THE ABDUCTION FROM THE SERAGLIO. *1781/82*

You know that I am an out-and-out Englishman.

Mozart to his father, October 19th 1782

Archbishop Colloredo particularly came into Mozart's thoughts when the singer of Osmin was chosen ... In Osmin revenge is palpably taken ... Mozart is more likely to have identified himself with his heroine (in her attitude of defiance) than thought of his fiancée.

Michael Levey, THE LIFE AND DEATH OF MOZART *(Weidenfeld & Nicolson, 1971)*

I

IN JANUARY 1778 Leopold Mozart received a letter from his son, Wolfgang, now just twenty-two, giving him news of a visit to Caroline, Princess of Orange, at Kirchheim, in southern Germany, and also of his introduction to Aloysia Weber, a pretty girl of seventeen with a beautiful voice.

Mannheim. January 17th 1778

Next Wednesday I am going for a few days to Kirchheim-Bolanden to visit the Princess of Orange. People here have said such nice things to me about her that I have at last decided to go. A Dutch officer, a good friend of mine, got a terrible scolding from her for not bringing me with him when he went to offer her his New Year wishes. I shall get eight louis d'or at least, for, as she is passionately fond of singing, I have had four arias copied for her. As she has a nice little orchestra and gives a concert every day, I shall also present her with a symphony.

The copying of the arias will not cost me much, for it has been done by a certain Herr Weber, who is accompanying me there. He has a daughter who sings admirably and has a lovely, pure voice; she is only fifteen [seventeen in fact]. She lacks dramatic action; were it not for that, she might be the prima donna on any stage. Her father is a thoroughly honest German, who is bringing up his children well, and for that very reason the girl is persecuted with attentions here. He has six children, five girls* and one son. He and his wife and children have been obliged to live for fourteen years on an income of 200 gulden and, because he has always attended carefully to his duties and has provided the Elector with a very talented singer, he now gets in all – 400 gulden. She sings most excellently my aria

* Only four daughters have been identified.

written for De Amicis [in *Lucio Silla*], with those horribly difficult passages, and she is to sing it at Kirchheim-Bolanden.

The first part of this letter, about the Princess, was the kind of information that Leopold wanted to hear; he told his son that 'you must now endeavour to make greater strides, to win for yourself, glory, honour and a great name.' The second part, about the Webers, was another matter. The sooner he left them the better. Leopold urged him to go back to Paris, one of the musical capitals of the world and where he would be fêted and would make money. But even there would be dangers, he told his son – dangers that Leopold must have thought about when he read of Wolfgang's admiration and love for the attractive Aloysia. Without delay he put pen to paper and wrote to his son:

> Count Kühnburg, Chief Equerry, who, as is well known, lays no claim to saintliness, talked to me a few days ago and expressed extreme anxiety about Paris, which he knows thoroughly. He said that you should be on your guard against its dangers and that you should refrain from all familiarity with young Frenchmen, and even more so with the women, who are always on the look-out for strangers to keep them, who run after young people of talent in an astonishing way in order to get at their money, draw them into their net, or even to land them as husbands. God and your own good sense will preserve you. Any such calamity would be the death of me!

It is easy to understand Leopold's anxieties. Any father worries about his child's future and Wolfgang, he knew, was a genius. This had been obvious since the age of six when his mastery of the keyboard had delighted the courts of Europe. One rash liaison could well jeopardise his son's future.

But Wolfgang was delighted with his new friends, the Webers, and their four daughters, Josefa, Aloysia, Constanze and Sophie. This delight was expressed in a doggerel verse he wrote to his mother:

January 31st 1778

Oh, mother mine!
Butter is fine.
Praise and thanks be to Him,
We're alive and full of vim.
Through the world we dash,
Though we're short of cash.
But we don't find this provoking
And none of us is choking ...
Wendling, no doubt, is in a rage
That I haven't composed a single page;
But when I cross the Rhine once more,
I'll surely dash home through the door
And, lest he call me mean and petty,
I'll finish off his four quartetti.*

The concerto† for Paris I'll keep, 'tis more fitting...
Indeed I swear 'twould be far better fun
With the Webers around the world to run...

Your faithful child,
With distemper wild.
Trazom

Their visit to Princess Caroline of Orange was a great success. Mozart, already a veteran traveller, called it airily 'just a holiday trip, nothing more'. His admired Aloysia Weber sang her arias excellently; he had got to know her properly, he told his father in a letter, and had 'discovered her great powers'. In this part of the world, at Kirchheim, he was in a musical paradise: 'they have only three hundred concerts in the year.' Mozart gave a dozen piano recitals and presented four of his symphonies to his hostess; and Aloysia sang thirteen songs and played some of his piano sonatas, which even he considered difficult to perform. These she played at sight, slowly but without a single mistake. He was not paid as much as he expected, but was glad to make a profit of 42 gulden on the visit.

* Johann Wendling had secured for Mozart a commission to write three flute concertos and two flute quartets.
† Flute Concerto in G, 1778 (K. 313).

Having pleased his father with a favourable report on this holiday trip, he followed it up in the same letter with his next plan, an ambitious continental tour with the Webers. The delightful Kirchheim interlude was rapidly reaching an alarming climax. He was going to make a musical and social partnership with Aloysia Weber and her father. Everything seemed to him set for success. What is more, the sum of 200 gulden had been promised by a rich Dutchman, de Jean,* for the composition of 'three short concertos and a couple of concertos for the flute'. Herr Weber promised to act as his agent, procuring engagements for recitals and concerts, and a trip to Italy with Aloysia and her father would follow. Having since childhood received instructions in plenty from his father, Mozart now offered some in return.

> My advice [to the Webers] is that they should go to Italy. So now I should like you to write to your good friend Lugiati, and the sooner the better, and enquire what are the highest terms given to a prima donna in Verona – the more the better, one can always climb down – perhaps too it would be possible to obtain the Ascensa [an opera contract for the church festival of the Ascension] in Venice. As far as her singing is concerned, I would wager my life that she will bring me renown. Even in a short time she has greatly profited by my instruction, and how much greater will the improvement be by then! I am not anxious about her acting. If our plan succeeds, we, M. Weber, his two daughters [Josefa and Aloysia] and I will have the honour of visiting my dear Papa and my dear sister for a fortnight on our way through Salzburg. I beg you to do your best to get us to Italy. You know my greatest desire is – to write operas ... I envy anyone who is composing one ... The thought of helping a poor family, without injury to myself, delights my very soul.   [February 4th 1778]

Anna Maria, Mozart's mother, who was with him at this time in Mannheim, summed up the situation succinctly: 'When Wolfgang makes new acquaintances, he immediately wants to give his life and property for them.' In Wolfgang's

* Ferdinand de Jean (1731–97), amateur flautist, a ship's surgeon in the Dutch East India Company, who had made a fortune in the East Indies.

opinion Herr Weber resembled Leopold, 'and the whole family resemble the Mozarts ... I have nothing to worry about; I found my torn clothes mended; in short, I was waited on like a Prince.'

Leopold, in the same letter, was informed that his impetuous son planned to take the Webers to Switzerland and perhaps also to Holland. 'The eldest daughter [Josefa] will be very useful to us; for we could have our own *ménage*, as she can cook.' The possibility that Wolfgang would be trapped into marriage by a poor girl was already assuming the outlines of reality before the trip to France had begun. To Leopold, Wolfgang's future must have seemed horribly clear. Although Aloysia was a talented singer, she was only seventeen and one of a large impoverished family. Wolfgang was sublimely indifferent to the difficulties of procuring engagements in Italy, and would end up spending any money he received on Herr Weber's children.

While this disturbing letter was on its way to Leopold in Salzburg, he was writing to Wolfgang imploring him to be exceedingly careful in Paris with everyone he met. On his own two earlier visits to Paris (in 1763 and 1766), he reminded his son:

> I avoided all acquaintances, and, mark you, *particularly all familiarity with people of our own profession*; you will remember that I did the same in Italy. I made the acquaintance and sought only the friendship of people of position – and, what is more, among those I associated with older people, never with young fellows, not even if they were of the highest rank ... You are but a young man of twenty-two; so you cannot have that settled gravity which might discourage any young fellow, of whatever rank he may be, an adventurer, jester or deceiver, old or young ... One drifts imperceptibly into these traps, and then one cannot get out. I shall say nothing about women, for where they are concerned, the greatest reserve and prudence are necessary, Nature herself being our enemy. Whoever does not use his judgement to the utmost to keep the necessary reserve with them, will exert it in vain later on when he endeavours to extricate himself from the labyrinth, *a misfortune which very often ends in death.*

Four days later – still in ignorance of his son's plans – Leopold wrote another long letter, full of good advice and pleas for caution. He gave Wolfgang the names of several musicians – a clavierist, a violinist, a harpist ('a cheerful fool'), a conceited cellist, two singers and a lutenist – and three composers, Gluck, Piccinni and Grétry. But even these professional people, with whom Mozart would obviously have something in common, were to be treated with care. 'With very few exceptions,' declared his father, 'you will gain nothing by associating with these people ... *De la politesse et pas d'autre chose.* You can always be perfectly natural with people of high rank; but with everybody else *please behave like an Englishman.*'

It is easy to understand how Leopold felt when he discovered what his son had been up to in Mannheim. This close involvement with the Weber family, and marriage to Aloysia, would end in disaster. He read the news 'with amazement and horror. The whole night long I was unable to sleep and am so exhausted that I can only write quite slowly, word by word...'

Salzburg, February 11th 1778

Merciful God! Suddenly you strike up a new acquaintanceship with Herr Weber. Now *this* family is the most honourable, the most Christian family, and the daughter is to have the leading role in the tragedy to be enacted between your own family and hers! ... You are thinking of taking her to Italy as a prima donna. Tell me, do you know of any prima donna who, without having first appeared many times in Germany, has walked on to the stage in Italy as prima donna? ... I am quite willing to believe that Mlle. Weber sings like a Gabrielli; that she has a *powerful voice* for the Italian stage; that she has the build of a prima donna and all the rest; but it is absurd of you to vouch for her capacity to act. Acting calls for more than these qualities. One must have a stage presence ... As for your proposal to travel about with Herr Weber and his two daughters, it has nearly made me lose my reason! ... a horrible idea! Could you really make up your mind to go trailing about the world with strangers? Conditions are now such that it is impossible to

guess where war may break out, for everywhere regiments are
either on the march or under marching orders ... *Off with you to
Paris!* and that soon! In Paris you will see a refined manner of
life, which forms an astonishing contrast to the coarseness of
our German courtiers and their ladies; and there you may
become proficient in the French tongue ... I am going to tell
you what you *can* do for Mlle. Weber. Has Signor Raaff heard
her sing? Have a word with him and ask him to hear her
perform her arias ... If she impresses him, she can count on
making a good impression on all the Italian impresarios who
knew him in his prime. Meanwhile she could surely find an
opportunity of getting on the stage in Mannheim, where, even
if it is unpaid work, she could be gaining experience ... Hurt
me now, if you can be so cruel! Win fame and *make money* in
Paris; then, *when you have money to spend*, go off to Italy and get
commissions for operas ... Then you could put forward Mlle.
Weber's name, which can be the more easily done if you do so
personally ... Nannerl [Wolfgang's sister] has wept her full
share during these last two days.

Leopold had a graphic view of his son's possible fate as an
impoverished musician. 'Utterly forgotten by the world, cap-
tured by some woman,' he wrote, 'you will die bedded on
straw in an attic full of starving children.' His anxiety was
justified to some extent but he could see his son's future only in
extremes: success and glory or misery and starvation. To
marry the daughter of a poor musician was a recipe for disaster. What he hoped for was a suitable marriage to some charming girl, possibly a member of the aristocracy with sufficient
money to relieve Wolfgang of financial worries.

So far Leopold had enjoyed complete authority over his
brilliant son but now he found his position flouted. To make
matters worse, he heard unfavourable reports about the most
important member of the Weber family, the mother. Wolfgang was soon to divulge that she drank too much and even
encouraged her children to drink wine.

Political events in Europe can have done nothing to allay
Leopold's worries. War and rumours of war were spreading in

central and eastern Europe. The powerful despots of Austria, Prussia and Russia were turning greedily towards Poland. In 1763, Augustus III had died and Russian troops marched into the country, installing Stanislas Poniatowski as king. Nine years later, alarmed by his reforms, the Russians again invaded Poland, pushing the country's western boundary forward by one hundred miles. But both Frederick of Prussia and Joseph of Austria were looking eastward for possible gains and between them, the three states seized a quarter of Poland and nearly half her population.

The death of Maximilian Joseph of Bavaria in 1777, gave the Austrian Emperor another opportunity for aggression but Frederick of Prussia resisted Joseph's claim and the territory – just across the Salzburg border – was engulfed in an absurd conflict, the War of the Bavarian Succession, which ended with the Treaty of Teschen in 1779. Austria was humiliated but Prussia was left 25 million crowns the poorer. Throughout Mozart's last years, central Europe was thus racked by war while France was heading towards revolution. In 1793, only two years after his death, France was at war with Great Britain and her armies marched into the Netherlands, Spain, Italy, Egypt and Prussia. In 1809, Salzburg disappeared as an independent state and was incorporated into the dukedom of Bavaria. Leopold Mozart's fears for his son's future and for the stability of his country were certainly understandable.

'You want everything to be done at once, before people have seen you or heard any of your works,' Leopold complained. 'I shall have the arias which you want for Mlle. Weber copied, and I shall send what I can find.' Aloysia's singing, Wolfgang told his father in reply, 'goes to the heart ... Raaff himself (who is certainly no flatterer), when asked to give his candid opinion, said "She sang, not like a student, but like a master."'

If Mozart had not been at this stage of his life a conscientious Catholic, and if he had been more like his fellow musicians, Aloysia would perhaps have become his mistress. He admitted that this was a possibility in another letter to his father.

Mannheim, February 22nd 1778

I feel no inclination to write today. It is impossible to put on paper all that we think – at least I find it so. Please believe what you like of me, but not anything bad. There are people who think that no-one can love a poor girl without having evil designs; and that charming word *maîtresse*, whore in our tongue, is really much too charming. But I am no Brunetti!* no Mysliwecek [another composer]! I am a Mozart; and a young and clean-minded Mozart. So you will forgive me, I hope, if in my eagerness I sometimes get excited, though I would much rather say, if I sometimes write naturally. I have much to say on this subject, but I cannot; for I find it impossible to do so . . . I have made up my mind to stay at home today, because it is snowing so hard. Tomorrow I must go out, for our house nymph, Mlle. Pierron, my highly esteemed pupil, is to scramble through my concerto [K. 246, written in 1776 for Countess Lutzow] at the French concert which is held every Monday. I too, prostitution though it be, shall ask them to give me something to strum and shall contrive to thump it out *prima fista* . . . Now please let me stop, for I am not at all in the humour for writing letters today, but feel far more inclined to compose.

Reading this letter, Leopold Mozart might well have had mixed feelings. If his son was resisting any possible temptations that might exist to make Aloysia his mistress, might this not make it more likely that he would marry her? Wolfgang's mother, Anna Maria, did little to allay his fears as her next letter reveals:

Most people here [in Mannheim] have no religion. They are out-and-out free-thinkers. The whole household [of Herr Wendling, with whom Wolfgang had been planning to travel to Paris] knows nothing about religion and does not value it. The mother and the daughter never go to church from one end of the year to the other, never go to confession and never hear mass. On the other hand they are always going off to the theatre. They say that a church is not healthy. No-one knows

* The Archbishop of Salzburg's first violinist.

that this is the reason why Wolfgang has not gone off with
them, for, if it were known, we should be laughed at. Even our
Privy Court Councillor, who is a bird of the same feather, does
not know it ... I do hope that Wolfgang will make his fortune
in Paris quickly, so that you and Nannerl may follow us soon.
How delighted I should be to have you both with us, for
nothing could be better. If it is God's will, He will arrange it.

Leopold was delighted when his son did not go to Paris with
the Wendlings. Their daughter, Auguste, had become the
mistress of the ruler of the Palatinate, the Elector. It would not
have surprised the aristocracy or the musicians at Mannheim if
their young friend, Mozart, had also taken a mistress, especially if she were an attractive and promising young singer, like
Aloysia Weber. Leopold informed his wife and son that he
could not shake off his worries, and that they were giving him
nervous palpitations. His son was fully aware of his own
genius, but his father spelt out the position clearly:

Salzburg, February 23rd 1778

Millions have not received the tremendous favour which God
has bestowed upon you. What a responsibility! And what a
tragedy if such a great genius were to founder! That can happen
in a moment. You are confronted with far more dangers than
those millions who have no talent, for you are exposed to many
more ordeals and temptations ... By the next post I shall send
you all the addresses you require and also letters to Diderot,
d'Alembert and the rest.

If Leopold was anxious to get his son away from Aloysia
Weber and to find fame in Paris, Wolfgang and his mother
were now worried about Leopold's safety in Salzburg. If the
Austrian army was going to invade Bavaria, this could mean
the outbreak of war. If Prussia and perhaps Russia took up
arms to protect Bavaria's independence, Salzburg might well
be attacked in the ensuing conflict. 'If war should break out,'
wrote Mozart to his father, 'follow us at once, I beg you.' Two

months later, Leopold was reporting to his son: 'We must wait and see what the situation in Germany is going to be. The whole country is full of soldiers, and there is no talk of anything but the delivery of horses and the transport of food. In Prussia and Austria people are being whipped off the streets and pulled out of their beds to be turned into soldiers . . . Paris is the safest place to live in.'

Before Mozart and his mother finally left Mannheim for Paris, he praised Aloysia once more in a letter to his father, and gave him a clear indication of what the next step in the romance was going to be.

Mannheim, March 7th 1778

Monsieur
mon très cher Père

I am very much obliged to you for all the trouble you have taken about the arias [copied for him and sent to Mannheim]. *Next to God comes Papa* was my motto or axiom as a child, and I still cling to it. Mlle. Weber well deserves your kindness. I only wish you could hear her sing my new aria [K. 294]. I say, hear her sing it, for it is absolutely made for her. A man like you who really understands what portamento singing is,* would certainly find complete satisfaction in her performance. Once I am happily settled in Paris and, as I hope, our circumstances with God's help have improved and we are all more cheerful and in better spirits, I shall tell you my thoughts more fully and ask you for a great favour. I have set all my hopes on Paris, for the German princes are all skinflints.

In other words, Mozart was saying that he loved Aloysia so much that success in Paris would encourage him to ask her to marry him. Leopold must have hoped that in France distance and fame would lend his son not enchantment, but caution and second thoughts.

Neither distance nor acclaim ousted Aloysia Weber from Mozart's thoughts in Paris. Two days before he left Mannheim, she took part in an afternoon concert, as one of the three soloists in a performance of his Concerto for Three

---

* Singing each note in between the two notes indicated in the score.

Pianos (K. 242, composed in 1776) and also sang two of his arias. With the latter, referred to in the letter just quoted, she did herself and Mozart 'indescribable honour, for everyone said that no aria had ever affected them as did this one ... The members of the orchestra never ceased praising the aria and talking about it. I have many friends in Mannheim (people of position and means), who wished very much to keep me there.' Aloysia also knitted two pairs of mittens for him, and her father presented him with a set of Molière's comedies. At a farewell visit the night before he left for Paris, 'they all wept' at his departure.

We have only one letter from Mozart to Aloysia during the six months he spent in Paris. In this long letter dated July 30th and written in Italian, he asked her not to make him suffer too long, waiting for a letter from her; and he tells her about the recitative and aria he is writing for her, composed to words taken from Gluck's opera *Alceste*, entitled 'Popoli di Tessaglia' (K. 316), saying candidly that 'I can only say that of all my compositions of this kind, this scena is the best I have ever composed.' This work is indeed brilliant and one which gives a great soprano one glorious opportunity after another to reveal both her skill and her character.

The day before Mozart wrote to Aloysia, he wrote an even longer letter, of nearly three thousand words, to her father, telling him he would do all he could to help him if he and his family moved to Paris. The letter is full of suggestions for furthering Aloysia's career; but, while genuinely offering help, Mozart with equal honesty explains how difficult life might be for them:

> You have no idea what a dreadful time I am having here. Everything goes so slowly; and until one is well known, nothing can be done in the matter of composition ... Give my best greetings to your wife, and to all your loved ones; and rest assured that I shall use every effort to help you to improve your position. If I hadn't a father and a sister, to whom I must sacrifice everything and whom I must try to support, I would completely renounce my own interests with the greatest

pleasure – and consult your interests only. For your welfare –
your pleasure – your happiness are the very foundation of
mine.

                              Farewell, your constant Mozart.

Four weeks before this letter was written, Mozart's mother,
Anna Maria, had died of some kind of fever. Mozart broke the
tragic news to his father in two letters full of wisdom, compas-
sion and a most moving attempt at consolation. The first letter
was a marvellous example of considerate deception. To save
his father the full shock of this completely unexpected news,
he pretended that she was still alive, but seriously ill. Six days
later he told him the full story. These two letters, together with
another which he wrote to the Abbé Bullinger, a family friend
in Salzburg, asking him to comfort his father, should be read in
their entirety, not only as unsurpassed examples of letters of
commiseration but also as a perfect revelation of Mozart's true
character. His composure, his suffering, his own sorrow and
his awareness of the grief of his father and sister in Salzburg,
are all expressed with astonishing clarity, as is his stoically
Christian acceptance of death as simply a temporary parting.

In another letter to Bullinger he told him that he felt sure
that some day his father would not 'deny me a request on
which the whole happiness and peace of my life depend and
which will certainly be quite fair and reasonable'. He had
already told his father how he had recommended 'my beloved
Mlle. Weber' to the distinguished tenor Anton Raaff, who
agreed that she was very talented. Leopold was still finding
this continued devotion to Aloysia and the other members of
the Weber family somewhat irksome.

You are forever writing about the embarrassed circumstances
of the Webers. But tell me, how, if you have any common
sense, can you entertain the idea that you could be the person
capable of making the fortune of these people? . . . We may of
course make an effort to assist Mlle. Weber as far as possible and
even in due course achieve all you desire; but are our resources
sufficient to succour a family with six children? Who can do

this? – I? – You? You, who have not yet been able to help your family? How can you help others before you have helped yourself? You write: 'I commend them to you with all my heart. If only they could enjoy an income of a thousand gulden even for a few years.' My dearest son! When I read that, could I help fearing for your reason? Great God! . . . Where, pray, are the courts, where is there a single court, which will give a thousand gulden to a singer? In Munich they get five, six or at most seven hundred gulden, and do you imagine that someone is going to give a thousand gulden forthwith to a young person, who is considered a beginner? . . . All your thoughts and cares for Herr Weber, and mine too, are absolutely futile until you are in a better position; and that must be your main object.   [July 3rd 1778]

Only four days later Leopold was able to tell his son that the Archbishop of Salzburg had invited him back to Salzburg as *Konzertmeister* with a salary of 500 gulden a year, and was going to pay Leopold the same amount. 'So together we shall receive *an official salary* of 1,000 gulden a year.' What is more, Wolfgang would be free to travel where he liked 'for the purpose of composing an opera. In Salzburg you will be midway between Munich, Vienna and Italy. My next letter will tell you that you are to leave. We can hardly wait for the hour and the moment when we shall see you. I shall revive when you are here.'

Mozart had not had the acclaim in Paris that his father had forecast, but that was not surprising. As Leopold himself pointed out, Gluck, the leading composer in Paris, had not become famous until he was approaching forty, while Mozart was still only twenty-two. Indeed Mozart was already begin-ning to establish himself. 'My affairs,' he told his father in August, four months after his arrival in Paris, 'are beginning to improve steadily, and I do not doubt that if I could make up my mind to hold out here for a few years, I should certainly get on very well. I am now fairly well known or – rather people know me, even if I don't know *them*. I have made a name for myself by my two symphonies [K. 297 and perhaps K. 311a], the second of which was performed on the 8th [three days earlier].' Only seven weeks after arriving in Paris he was offered the post of organist at Versailles, at a salary of 2,000 livres a year. He would have to spend only half the year at Versailles and go where he liked for the other six months. This salary was the equivalent of 915 gulden, but he turned it down, in spite of the many advantages. The reason could not have been a real desire to return to his father in Salzburg, as he detested the town, feelings which he expressed openly in letters to his father and to Bullinger.* Salzburg, he explained candidly, 'is no place for my talent'. Injustices which his father and he had endured there were enough 'to make us wish to forget such a place and blot it out of our memory for ever!'

It was therefore not Salzburg that lured him away from Paris, nor even his father and sister, as he was about to demonstrate by taking nearly four months, from September to mid-January, to travel to his home town. If the Webers were still at Mannheim, he told his father, he would like the pleasure of going there to visit them. 'When I return to Salzburg,' he declared, 'I shall certainly not fail to plead with great enthusiasm for my dear friend.' If it had not been for his love of Aloysia, he might have stayed on in Paris, for his father was correct in his estimation of the importance of this town as a thriving musical centre for the whole of Europe. In the *Almanach Musical* of 1783 we read that here were 194 composers, 63 singing teachers, 93 violin teachers, 42 cello instructors, 12 organ makers and 32 music engravers.

The Parisians took immediately to his sparkling *Paris* symphony (no. 32); the audience, he told his father, 'were quite carried away – and there was a tremendous burst of applause.' At one stage they even shouted for a replay at the end of the first movement – 'there were shouts of "*Da Capo*" . . . I was so happy that, as soon as the symphony was over, I went off to the Palais Royal, where I had a large ice and said a rosary as I had vowed to do, and went home.' A week before this exciting event another composition of his was performed at the Paris

* August 7th, September 11th 1778, January 8th 1779.

Opera House, music for a ballet entitled *Les Petits Riens*, consisting of thirteen orchestral pieces. At one stage in this ballet, we read in the *Journal de Paris* (of June 12th) that a shepherdess, disguised as a man, puts an end to the attempts of two other shepherdesses to make love to her, by baring her breast. This also was well received by the audience. 'At the moment where Mlle. Asselin enlightens the two girls, several voices cried *bis*.'

Mozart's four months journey from Paris to his father and sister in Salzburg, and his correspondence with Leopold, reveal the climax of his attachment and devotion to Aloysia. But she was not in love with him, and this he only realised at the end of December, when he came to stay with the Webers, who had by this time moved to Munich. Perhaps all along he was afraid that he would be rejected, and this might have caused him to spin out his return to Salzburg as much as possible. After the death of his mother in July, Mozart, now aged twenty-three, was experiencing for the first time both the exhilaration and the drawbacks of independence and freedom. He had gone to Paris to please his father; he was now returning to Salzburg at his command. In Paris, and now in Strasbourg and Mannheim, he had been applauded and appreciated; people there had loved and admired him, both as a composer and as a man. Strasbourg, where he gave one recital and two concerts, was

loth to let me go! You cannot think how they esteem and love me here. They say that everything about me is so distinguished – that I am so composed – and polite – and have such excellent manners. Everyone knows me. As soon as they heard my name, the two Herren Silbermann and Herr Hepp, the organist, came to call on me, and also *Kapellmeister* Richter. The latter now lives very economically, for instead of forty bottles of wine a day, he only swills about twenty. [In Mannheim] there is a regular scramble to invite me. In a word, Mannheim loves me, as I love Mannheim ... I feel the greatest pleasure at the thought of paying you a visit – but only annoyance and anxiety when I see myself back at that beggarly court!

As the weeks went by, Leopold was becoming frantic, still fearing that his son was going to marry Aloysia. In November he told Wolfgang that he 'was not at all opposed' to his love of Mlle. Weber, but this statement somehow lacks conviction. When he wrote this, he was wondering when his son would eventually return. 'I don't know what to say to you. I shall go mad or die of a decline,' he wrote despairingly. At the end of December, with still no definite promise from his son, he was understandably exasperated:

> Good God! How often have you made a liar of me! I am heartily ashamed of having assured everyone that you would quite certainly be home by Christmas or the New Year at the very latest. I am heartily sick of composing these long letters and during the last fifteen months have almost written myself blind. Am I to take the mail coach myself and fetch you? Surely my son will not let things reach such a pitch! ... People are saying to my face that you are treating the Archbishop – and, what is worse, your own father – as a fool.*

All Leopold's fears that his son would marry Herr Weber's daughter, Aloysia, were brought to an end by the girl herself. A conscientious worrier and pessimist, Leopold had not, it seems, envisaged the possibility that Aloysia was not in love with Wolfgang and would turn him down. In despair Mozart wrote to his father at the end of December saying that he was too miserable to write a proper letter. 'Today I can only weep. I have far too sensitive a heart ... A Happy New Year! I cannot manage anything more to-day.'

In October of the following year Aloysia married an actor, Joseph Lange, the first man to act the part of Hamlet in Vienna. He was also a painter and he has given us the most attractive portrait of Mozart, an unfinished work, but one which, more than any other, shows us not only the appearance but also the spirit of his genius. The clavier on which Mozart is playing has not been painted in but is easily imagined. Likewise the music comes silently to life. After some fifteen years together Aloysia

* Letters, November 19th, December 28th, 31st 1778.

and Joseph Lange were to part. Mozart continued to love her, and wrote seven magnificent concert arias for her, all of which give us a clear indication of her vocal range and technique.* She sang at his concerts, took part in a pantomime, as Colombine with Mozart as Harlequin, in the Vienna carnival of 1783, and sang one of the leading roles in his opera, *Der Schauspieldirektor (The Impressario)*. Her husband also painted a portrait of Constanze in 1782, which perhaps is as successful as his portrait of Mozart in revealing something of her character.

Mozart may have seen a production of *Hamlet* in Salzburg, on October 13th 1780, when the company of Emanuel Schikaneder presented this play, in F. W. L. Schröder's translation. In the following month he justifiably criticised one detail in the text of the drama: 'If the speech of the Ghost in *Hamlet* were not so long, it would be far more effective ... The audience [in *Idomeneo*] must believe that the subterranean voice really exists. How can this effect be produced if the speech is too long?' As Brigid Brophy points out in *Mozart, the Dramatist*, his arias can be compared to Hamlet-like soliloquies; and ghostly voices play an important role in *Idomeneo* and *Don Giovanni*. After his death, Constanze told two visitors from England, Mary and Vincent Novello, that he had indeed read some of the Shakespeare plays.

For two years harmony reigned between Mozart and his father but in March 1781 Wolfgang was summoned by his employer, Hieronymus Colloredo, Archbishop of Salzburg, to join the episcopal household in Vienna, where the Weber family were now living. Within two months, he left not only the room put at his disposal at the German House, the headquarters of the Teutonic Order, but also his Court appointment as organist – and rented a room in Frau Weber's flat. 'Old Madame Weber has been good enough to take me into her house, where I have a pretty room,' he told his father. 'Moreover, I am living with people who are obliging and who supply me with all the things which one often requires in a

* K. 294, 316, 383, 416, 418, 419 and 538, composed between 1778 and 1788.

hurry and which one cannot have when one is living alone.' He said good-bye to his regular income of 450 gulden a year and was once again associating with a family disliked by his father. Aloysia Weber had chosen to marry another man, but there were three other unmarried daughters in the house. Mozart must have known how his father would react to this sudden change in his son's career and his sudden exposure to the dangers of both poverty and marriage to one of the Weber girls.

Mozart himself, in December of this year, described Aloysia, now married, as 'a false, malicious person and a coquette'. The eldest girl, Josefa, was 'a lazy, gross, perfidious woman, and as cunning as a fox.' The youngest, Sophie, was 'still too young to be anything in particular. She is just a good-natured, but feather-headed creature! May God prevent her from seduction!' As for Cäcilie Weber, their mother, now widowed, Wolfgang admitted some remark of his father's about her, saying it was 'justified only in so far as she likes wine, more so, I admit, than a woman ought to. I have never seen her drunk, and it would be a lie if I were to say so. The children only drink water – and, although their mother almost forces wine upon them, she cannot induce them to touch it. This often leads to a lot of wrangling. Can you imagine a mother quarrelling with her children about such a matter?' All these candid comments were in letters to his father.

The remaining daughter, Constanze, likewise did not escape Mozart's critical eye. Leopold, already stunned by Wolfgang's foolhardy rejection of the Archbishop's patronage, was given an unflattering description of her. Less than three months after moving in with the Webers, Mozart wrote to his father that he was thinking of moving to another house, 'solely because people are gossiping'. The rumour was that he was going to marry Constanze. But 'if ever there was a time when I thought less of getting married, it is most certainly now!' declared Mozart, perhaps with complete sincerity. Who was spreading this ridiculous rumour? Could it have been Frau Weber? Mozart was now composing *The Abduction from the Seraglio* and one might ask who, in the Weber apartment, was abducting whom? By mistake, in one of his letters, Mozart referred to this opera as *Die Verführung*, instead of *Die Entführung aus dem Serail*, the Seduction, instead of the Abduction. As Mozart now became increasingly committed – to judge by his own letters – to Constanze and her mother, the question now arises, who was seducing whom?

It is at this point in the story of the Weber family and Mozart that real doubts arise about what was really happening. Leopold, as a witness, has been silenced by Constanze's later destruction of his letters; we do not have a single letter by Constanze to Mozart or to his father;* and Mozart himself, in his letters to his father, leaves many questions unanswered. It is also hard to accept his detailed account of his dismissal by the Archbishop of Salzburg as the full story.

'I did not know,' he wrote, 'that I was a valet – that was the last straw. I ought to have idled away a couple of hours every morning in the antechamber. True, I was often told that I ought to present myself, but I never could remember that this was part of my duty, and I only turned up punctually whenever the Archbishop sent for me.' Once a day, at noon, he sat down to lunch with 'the valets, that is, the body and soul attendants of His Worship, the controleur, the confectioner, the two cooks,' two musicians, 'and my insignificant self. The two valets sit at the top of the table, but at least I have the honour of being placed above the cooks.' There was nothing unusual about such an arrangement, and it was no great hardship. Court composers and musicians were the servants of their employers and were all treated as such. Mozart had little to complain about, since he was fortunate enough to receive a regular salary, free food and lodging, for doing the only kind of work he enjoyed doing, that is composing. After only two months of this normal and surely tolerable existence, Mozart was accused by the Archbishop of being 'the most dissolute fellow that he knew'. He called Mozart a scoundrel, a rascal, a

* Apart from two short, uninformative postscripts added to letters from Mozart.

knave, a dissolute fellow and a vagabond. 'He,' Mozart tells us, 'blazed away like a fire. No-one served him so badly as I did.' Colloredo's final remark was that he 'will have nothing more to do with such a wretch'.

Mozart gives us a glimpse of the other side of the coin when he tells us that Archbishop Colloredo considered him 'a dreadfully conceited person'. This information came from Count Karl Arco, Chief Chamberlain to the Archbishop, who was so exasperated by Mozart that he kicked him out of the room at their final meeting. 'If he was so well disposed towards me,' declared Mozart, 'he ought to have reasoned quietly with me, rather than throw such words about as "clown" and "knave" and hoof a fellow out of the room with a kick on his arse.'

What was his father, what are we, to make of this abrupt termination of relations between two gifted and intelligent men, the political and religious ruler of Salzburg and the world's most Olympian composer? It is ridiculous to assume that Colloredo was a stupid philistine, with no understanding of Mozart's genius. Without his account of the *débâcle*, we are left to some extent in the dark. 'I am more highly respected in Vienna than he [Colloredo] is,' Mozart proudly told his father. 'He is only known as a presumptuous, conceited ecclesiastic, who despises every one here, whereas I am considered a very amiable person.' Leopold and Arco had exchanged letters about Wolfgang, and one can guess that they both felt exasperated; to his credit, the Archbishop never officially accepted Mozart's resignation.

Constanze and her mother played no part in this conflict but it sheds some light on the immediately ensuing drama – or tragedy, as Leopold regarded it – which culminated in Mozart's marriage to Constanze. Mozart has not given us a full picture of his resignation from court service, and now he proceeds to give an even sketchier account of his involvement with the Weber family. Every marriage is a private arrangement, in that only the couple concerned know fully their own feelings and motives. But with Mozart's courtship, betrothal and wedding, we cannot help sympathising with Leopold, who was totally opposed to it, even though he was persuaded to send his consent, which arrived the day after the wedding. Mozart had already shown himself to be highly critical of his fellow men and women. Fellow citizens of Salzburg, ecclesiastics, members of the aristocracy in France and Austria, composers and musicians and piano pupils in Vienna had all been severely and sometimes amusingly criticised by Wolfgang in his highly articulate letters. And now he was planning to marry a girl he himself described to his father as 'not ugly, but at the same time far from beautiful ... with some commonsense'. Taken by itself, this would be a half-hearted recommendation for a servant.

No parent could be blamed for finding such a statement disappointing and confusing. Wolfgang had already proved himself to be an aristocrat among composers and musicians, and mixing with the aristocracy he had always been at ease, while his fellow musicians preferred to stay in the background. Soon after his arrival in Vienna,

when we were to go to Prince Galitzin's, Brunetti [the violinist] said to me in his usual polite manner, 'You must be here at seven o'clock this evening, so that we may go together to Prince Galitzin's. Angerbauer [the valet] will take us there.' I replied: 'All right. But if I'm not here at seven o'clock sharp, just go ahead. You need not wait for me. I know where he lives and I will be sure to be there.' I went there alone on purpose, because I really feel ashamed to go anywhere with him. When I got upstairs, I found Angerbauer standing there to direct a lackey to show me in. But I took no notice, either of the valet or the lackey, but walked straight on through the rooms into the music room, for all the doors were open – and went straight up to the Prince [Archbishop Colloredo], and paid him my respects and stood there talking to him. I had completely forgotten my friends, Ceccarelli [the singer] and Brunetti, for they were not to be seen. They were leaning against the wall behind the orchestra, not daring to come forward a single step.

A man so brilliant, so charming and so attractive, could fall in love with the richest, most beautiful young woman in the capital.

Mozart was now twenty-five. He had felt strong enough to end his service with the Archbishop but he did not yet break free of his dependence on his father, although there were now increasingly pressing reasons for asserting his own individuality. In consequence, in his letters to his father we get an increasingly imperfect and confusing picture of his true state of mind. It is certainly difficult to assess the true feelings of Constanze herself. In July 1781, a month after his final break with the Archbishop, he gave his father the first warning that he might marry Constanze, when he told him he might move because 'people are gossiping'. In the same letter he admitted that he 'fooled about and had fun with her when time permits'. Having gone so far, he then claimed that this was of no importance: 'If I had to marry all those with whom I have jested, I should have two hundred wives at least.' Here we have a foretaste of Don Giovanni's score card of seductions. Fooling about and having fun is a pastime not without certain consequences for those in the most isolated communities. Someone in the public eye is even more susceptible to these consequences. 'When a letter has arrived in Vienna with only my name on it, it has been delivered to me,' Mozart told his sister at this time. He had been famous since the age of six and he remained in the spotlight until he died. He could confidently claim to his sister that if the opera he was now composing, *The Abduction from the Seraglio*, was successful, he would 'be as popular in Vienna as a composer as I am on the clavier'.

In the middle of December 1781, five months after his declaration that he had no intention of marrying anyone, he revealed to his father that he wanted to marry Constanze.

Here is this important letter. In it Mozart is surprisingly candid about sex; and it is interesting to see that he puts forward, as one of the main reasons for his decision to marry Constanze, his desire to experience the joy of sex for the first time, as his adherence to Christianity had so far inhibited him.

Vienna, December 15th 1781

Mon très cher Père!

Dearest father! How gladly would I have opened my heart to you long ago, but I was deterred by the reproaches you might have made to me *for thinking of such a thing at an unseasonable time* – although indeed thinking can never be unseasonable. Meanwhile I am very anxious to secure here a small but *certain* income, which, together with what chance may provide, will enable me to live here quite comfortably – and then – to marry!

You are horrified at the idea? But I entreat you, dearest, most beloved father, to listen to me. I have been obliged to reveal my intentions to you. You must, therefore, allow me to disclose to you my reasons, which, moreover, are very well founded. The voice of nature speaks as loud in me as in others, louder, perhaps, than in many a big, strong lout of a fellow. I simply cannot live as most young men do these days. In the first place, I have too great a love of my neighbour and too high a feeling of honour to seduce an innocent girl; and, in the third place, I have too much horror and disgust, too much dread and fear of diseases and too much care for my health to fool about with whores. So I can swear that I have never had relations of that sort with any woman.

If such a thing had occurred, I should not have concealed it from you; for, after all, to err is natural enough in a man, and to err *once* in this way would be mere weakness – although indeed I should not undertake to promise that if I had erred once in this way, I should stop short at one slip. However, I stake my life on the truth of what I have told you. I am well aware that this reason (powerful as it is) is not urgent enough. But owing to my disposition, which is more inclined to a peaceful and domesticated existence than to revelry, I, who from my youth up have never been accustomed to look after my own belongings, linen, clothes and so forth, cannot think of anything more necessary to me than a wife. I assure you that I am often obliged to spend unnecessarily, simply because I do not pay attention to things. I am absolutely convinced that I should manage better with a wife (on the same income which I have now) than I do myself. And how many useless expenses would be avoided! True, other expenses would have to be met, but one knows what they are and can be prepared for them – in short, one leads a well-ordered existence.

A bachelor, in my opinion, is only half alive. Such are my views and I cannot help it. I have thought the matter over and reflected sufficiently, and I shall not change my mind.

But who is the object of my love? Do not be horrified again, I entreat you. Surely not one of the Webers? Yes, one of the Webers – not Josefa, nor Sophie, but Constanze, the middle one. In no other family have I ever come across such differences of character. The eldest [Josefa] is a lazy, gross, perfidious woman, and as cunning as a fox. Mme. Lange [Aloysia] is a false, malicious person and a coquette. The youngest – is still too young to be anything in particular – she is just a good-natured, but feather-headed creature! May God protect her from seduction! But the middle one, my good, dear Constanze, is the martyr of the family, and, probably for that very reason, is the kindest-hearted, the cleverest and, in short, the best of them all. She makes herself responsible for the whole household, and yet in their opinion she does nothing right. Oh, my most beloved father, I could fill whole sheets with descriptions of all the scenes that I have witnessed in that house.

Before I cease to plague you with my chatter, I must make you better acquainted with the character of my dear Constanze. She is not ugly, but at the same time far from beautiful. Her whole beauty consists in two little black eyes and a pretty figure. She has no wit, but she has enough common sense to enable her to fulfil her duties as a wife and mother. It is a downright lie that she is inclined to be extravagant. On the contrary, she is accustomed to be shabbily dressed, for the little that her mother has been able to do for her children, she has done for the two others, but never for Constanze. True, she would like to be neatly and cleanly dressed, but not smartly, and most things that a woman needs she is able to make for herself; and she dresses her own hair every day. Moreover she understands housekeeping and has the kindest heart in the world. I love her and she loves me with all her heart. Tell me whether I could wish myself a better wife?

One thing I must tell you, which is that when I resigned the Archbishop's service, our love had not yet begun. It was born of her tender care and attentions when I was living in their

house. Accordingly, all that I desire is to have a small assured
income (of which, thank God, I have good hopes), and then I
shall never cease entreating you to allow me to rescue this poor
girl – and to make myself and her – and, if I may say so, all of us
very happy. For you surely are happy when I am? And you are
to enjoy one half of *my fixed income*. Please take pity on your
son! I kiss your hands a thousand times and am ever your most
obedient son,

W. A. Mozart

Only a week later came news that must have depressed
Leopold even further. Wolfgang had been told by Constanze's
guardian, Johann von Thorwart, that he could not see her
again unless he signed a marriage contract. He bound himself
to 'marry Mlle. Constanze Weber within the space of three
years. If it should prove impossible for me to do so owing to
my changing my mind, she should be entitled to claim from
me three hundred gulden *a year*.'*

What sort of a marriage is it when the man is asked to
commit himself to make an annual payment, for an
unspecified number of years, if he does not marry his girl
friend? Mozart tried to allay his father's fears by saying
'Nothing in the world could have been easier to write. For I
knew that I should never have to pay these three hundred
gulden, because I should never forsake her, and that even
should I be so unfortunate as to change my mind, I should be
only too glad to get rid of her for three hundred gulden, while
Constanze, if I knew her, would be too proud to let herself be
sold.' Each sentence is surprising and confusing. The next step
in the drama was that Constanze tore up the contract. This had
the possibly calculated effect of making Mozart admire her all
the more.

The violinist, Peter von Winter, who also composed church
music and, later, nine operas, did what he could to persuade

---

* Frau Weber had also insisted that Aloysia's husband, Josef Lange, signed
a marriage contract, one which involved a regular payment to her even after
their marriage. Herr von Thorwart was the financial director of the National
Theatre in Vienna.

Mozart not to marry Constanze. 'You are a fool to get married,' he told him. 'Keep a mistress; you are earning enough money, you can afford it. What prevents you from doing so? That little bit of dirt called religion?' He also told him that Constanze was a slut. The word he used was *Luder*, which also means a whore. Mozart called him a beast, a liar and 'my worst enemy'.

Who was abducting whom? Who was seducing whom? Mozart was taking Constanze away from her mother but it was with her consent, indeed with her active encouragement; no force or fraud was employed by him. He was persuading Constanze to surrender her chastity, but only by promising to marry her. What part were Constanze and her mother playing? They were taking Mozart away from his state of bachelor independence by force, that is by encouraging, perhaps starting, rumours about his dalliance with Constanze, by the threat of legal action, in connection with the marriage contract, and, finally, by threatening to call in the police to bring Constanze home from the house of a mutual friend, where she was staying, unless he married her. As for seduction, Constanze and her mother were persuading him to surrender *his* chastity, at the same time, quite legitimately of course, insisting on marriage.

Leopold Mozart was so appalled and disgusted by Constanze's mother that he told his son that she 'should be put in chains, made to sweep streets and have boards hung round her neck with the words "seducer of youth".'

2

The Marriage of Mozart
1782

DON CURZIO   Marry her, or pay the two thousand pieces of gold she lent you.

FIGARO   I'm a gentleman, and without the consent of my parents ...

CHERUBINO   You who know the nature of love, ladies, see if I have it in my heart. I will tell you about my emotions. I cannot understand them. I freeze, and then I feel my soul aflame, and in the next moment, I turn cold again. I am drawn by something beyond myself – I don't know how to grasp it. I don't know what it may be.

FINAL CHORUS   Everyone will be happy now. This day of torments, of caprices and follies, is finished. Only love can end it in happiness and gaiety.

THE MARRIAGE OF FIGARO *1784/5*

2

CONSTANZE WEBER'S real feelings about Mozart are hard to assess. We only know what Mozart himself said about her in his letters to his father. In the opinion of one biographer, W. J. Turner, there is not enough evidence to satisfy us that she was truly in love with him. In other words, she tolerated him. Peter von Winter told Herr von Thorwart, Constanze's guardian, that Mozart had been 'far too intimate with her' (Mozart's own words in one of his letters) to the extent that, had the marriage not taken place, her reputation would have suffered. Mozart was unusually vituperative about von Winter, because of his attempt to discourage the marriage. He called him 'a beast in his ways of living and a child in the rest of his conduct. I shall not tell infamous truths about him in return for the infamous lies he has told about me.'

Whether or not to marry Mozart was not the only problem worrying Constanze. Her mother was not making life easy for her. When not playing at a concert, Mozart would spend the evening composing, from five or six till nine, and then he would 'go to my dear Constanze. But the joy of seeing one another is nearly always spoilt by her mother's bitter remarks. This is the reason why I am longing to be able to set her free and to rescue her as soon as possible. At half past ten or eleven, I come home – it depends on her mother's darts and on my capacity to endure them!' Then he might compose a little before going to bed. 'I often go on writing until one.' Some months earlier, Constanze had left her mother for a month, staying in another part of Vienna with Baroness von Waldstädten. She might have stayed longer, but the baroness fell ill, and now Frau Weber was refusing to let her stay there again.

Early in the new year, 1782, Mozart repeated his appeal to his father to give his blessing and consent to his marriage:

Vienna, January 9th 1782

Once more I implore you to be indulgent and merciful towards me. I never can be happy and contented without my dearest Constanze, and without your approval I shall only be so in part. So make me altogether happy, my dearest, most beloved father! I entreat you to do so.

We can glimpse some of the tensions in an earlier letter (December 22nd 1781) in which Mozart apologised to his father for having kept him in the dark so long. 'I hope you will forgive me, particularly as no-one has suffered more by the delay than I have. I would have written to you and disclosed everything, even if you had not provided the occasion for doing so in your last letter' – a letter which does not survive, thanks to Constanze. 'For, by Heaven,' Mozart continued, 'I could not have stood it – much – much longer.'

His love for Constanze was now common knowledge. Even the Emperor 'mentioned the marriage' after a recital that Mozart had given at the Palace of Schönbrünn, just outside Vienna. This recital took the form of a contest between him and Muzio Clementi, the famous pianist and composer, who lived for most of his life in London. Two pianofortes were assembled for the protagonists, but one of them was out of tune and three of the keys were stuck. 'That doesn't matter,' said the Emperor. After some polite conversation, the monarch asked Clementi to begin, airily addressing him, in Italian, as 'the Holy Catholic Church'. Both maestros played movements from some sonatas by Giovanni Paisiello and then improvised. The Emperor put his money on Mozart, in a wager with the Grand Duchess Maria of Russia, and won.

Mozart was understandably anxious not to alarm or depress his father still further, yet he openly depicted the worsening situation in the Weber household. Both Constanze and he had 'long ago observed her mother's designs. But the latter is very much mistaken, for she wishes us (when we marry) to live with her, as she has apartments to let. This is out of the question, for on no account would I consent to it, and my Constanze still less. *Au contraire*, she intends to see very little of her mother, and I shall do my best to stop it altogether, for we know her too well.' Mozart was convinced that Constanze was not like her mother; one was adorable, while the other was deplorable. His father remained unconvinced and told him so. In reply, Mozart implored him not to 'suspect my dear Constanze of harbouring such evil thoughts. Believe me, if she had such a disposition, I could not possibly love her. Dearest, most beloved father, my only wish is that we may soon meet, so that you may see her and – love her, for you love those who have kind hearts – that I know.'

As one Mozart biographer, Michael Levey, noted, *The Abduction from the Seraglio*, completed well before the marriage, 'cast its charm over reality, rather than vice-versa'. In January 1782 Mozart was able to report that, once some very necessary alterations had been made in the libretto and three important operas by Gluck had been performed, all would be ready for the production of his own opera. It would, he thought, be put on in the Royal Opera House, immediately after Easter. Gluck's operas were *Iphigenie in Tauris*, *Alceste* and *Orfeo*. Mozart had begun work on his opera in May 1781, when his escape from Archbishop Colloredo was building up to its climax. Further delays occurred, and then a date was fixed for the first performance in July. The success of his recent compositions and work on this new opera gave Mozart the courage not only to sever his connections with the Archbishop but also to stand up to his father's opposition to his marriage plans. The growing fame of the young composer was a spur not only to himself, in his conflict with the Archbishop and his father, but also to Frau Weber and Constanze. Leopold Mozart, with every justification, had longed for the day when his son would become the toast of Vienna, but he had not foreseen that fame very often produces its own surprises. His son was now firmly resolved to begin a new chapter in his life by marrying Constanze, in spite of the breach that this was already causing.

In March 1782, some three months after he had broken the news of his engagement, Mozart felt that he must do something to bring about some rapport between his father and sister in Salzburg and Constanze. He often sent Leopold a copy of his new compositions; sometimes the original manuscript, which his father would have copied. This time Mozart sent a rondo for piano and orchestra (K. 382) which he composed for an earlier piano concerto (K. 175, written in 1773). He had been playing this concerto in Vienna and, he tells us, 'it was making such a furore'. He had composed it specially for himself, he told his father, and no-one other than his sister must play it. He then went on to say that with this composition he was enclosing a snuff-box, which 'was quite pretty; the painting represents an English scene'. Also enclosed were a few watch-ribbons, which, he said, were then very much in fashion. From here it was an easy step to mention another present:

March 23rd 1782

I am sending my dear sister two caps in the latest Viennese fashion. Both are the handiwork of my dear Constanze. She sends her most devoted greetings to you and kisses your hands and also embraces my sister most affectionately, and asks her to forgive her if the caps are not as becoming as she would have wished, but the time was too short. Please return the hatbox by the next mail coach, for I borrowed it. So that the foolish thing may not travel all alone, be so good as to put the Rondo in again (after you have had it copied) ... My dear Constanze has surprised me this very moment and has just asked me whether she might dare to send my sister a little souvenir? At the same time I am to apologise for her, and to say that, as she is a poor girl, she has nothing to give – and that she hopes that my sister will take the will for the deed. The little cross is of no great value, but it is all the fashion in Vienna. But the little heart pierced by an arrow is something like my sister's heart with the arrow – and will please her better on that account.

A whole month went by before Constanze could be persuaded to follow up her present with a direct communication, a letter in her own hand. Mozart realised that this presented some problems, as he must have known that, receiving a letter from Constanze, Leopold would have a further cause for criticism. However, a letter, or a postscript from her added to his own letter, would, Mozart hoped, soften his father and sister – in spite of any shortcomings in spelling, vocabulary and grammar.

A letter from Mozart to Nannerl, his sister, would put her in a good mood perhaps, before reading Constanze's first communication.

Vienna, April 20th 1782

Dearest Sister!

My dear Constanze has at last summoned up courage to follow the impulse of her kind heart – that is, to write to you, my dear sister! Should you be willing to favour her with a reply (and indeed I hope you will, so that I may see the sweet creature's delight reflected on her face), may I beg you to enclose your letter to me? I only mention this as a precaution and so that you may know that her mother and sisters are not aware that she has written to you...

I kiss you a thousand times and remain your sincere brother

W. A. Mozart

Included in this letter is the only reference Mozart ever made about Constanze's interest in music. As this is the only mention, we cannot be sure of its veracity, especially when we take into account Mozart's understandable desire to present Constanze to his father in the most favourable light. She sang as one of the soloists in Wolfgang's *Mass in C Minor*, which he dedicated to her, at its first performance in St Peter's Church in Salzburg in 1783, and she also sang, perhaps in the chorus, in a performance of *La Clemenza di Tito* in Berlin in 1796; but we have the opinion of one contemporary, Adalbert Gyrowetz, who, in his autobiography, declared that she had a trembling voice. With the letter just quoted Mozart enclosed a prelude and fugue which he had just composed (Fantasy and Fugue in C major, K. 394). Constanze, he said, was 'really the cause of the fugue's coming into the world':

> Baron van Swieten, to whom I go every Sunday, gave me all the works of Handel and Sebastian Bach to take home with me (after I had played them to him). When Constanze heard the fugues, she absolutely fell in love with them. Now she will listen to nothing but fugues and particularly (in this kind of composition) the works of Handel and Bach. Well, as she had often heard me play fugues out of my head, she asked me if I had written any down, and when I said I had not, she scolded me roundly for not recording some of my compositions in this most artistic and beautiful of all musical forms, and never ceased to entreat me until I wrote down a fugue for her. So this is its origin.

We could not be surprised if Leopold and Nannerl took this with more than a grain of salt. After reading this introduction, they went on to read Nannerl's first letter from Constanze. It should be noted here that it cannot be literally translated; the shortcomings already mentioned were indeed there.

Vienna, April 20th 1782

Most honoured and valued friend!
　I should never have been so bold as to follow the wishes of my heart and to write to you, most esteemed friend, had not your brother assured me that you would not be offended by this step which I am taking only from a sincere longing to communicate, if only in writing, with a person, who, though unknown to me, is yet very precious, as she bears the name of Mozart – would you be angry if I dared to tell you that without knowing you in person I esteem you most highly just as the sister – of so worthy a brother and – love you – and dare to – ask for your friendship. Without being proud I say that I partly deserve it and shall try to Earn it wholly – may I offer you mine in return (which I have long since in my heart given to you) – o

yes! I Hope so – and in this hope I Remain, most honoured and valued friend, you most obedient servant and friend

Constanza Weber

please tell your papa that I kiss his hand.

If Constanze received a reply from Nannerl, it has not survived. A few days later, she decided – not for the first time – to tell Mozart that she could not marry him, for the simple reason, perhaps, that she did not love him. What discussions, what arguments led to this decision we do not know, but one letter of Mozart's gives us some indication of the verbal battles that may have taken place. We also learn that Constanze had on three occasions told Mozart that she would not marry him. If ever there was a good occasion for the marriage to have been called off, it was now. What is more, Mozart had something to complain about concerning Constanze's behaviour at a party, when, in his opinion, she had acted disgracefully. Only Mozart's determination to persevere with his plan kept their relationship alive. He wrote to Constanze:

Vienna, April 29th 1782

Dearest, most beloved Friend!

Surely you will still allow me to address you by this name? Surely you do not hate me so much that I may be your friend no longer, and you – no longer mine? Even if you will not be my friend any longer, yet you cannot forbid me to wish you well, my friend, since it has become very natural for me to do so. Do think over what you have said to me today.

In spite of all my entreaties you have thrown me over three times, and told me to my face that you intend to have nothing more to do with me. I (to whom it means more than it does to you to lose the object of my love) am not so hot-tempered, so rash and so senseless as to accept my dismissal. I love you far too well to do so. I entreat you, therefore, to ponder and reflect upon the cause of all this unpleasantness, which arose from my being annoyed that you were so impudently inconsiderate as to say to your sisters – and, be it noted, in my presence – that you had let a young man measure the calves of your legs. No woman who cares for her honour can do such a thing. It is quite a good maxim to do as one's company does. At the same time, there are many other factors to be considered – as, for example, whether only intimate friends and acquaintances are present – whether I am a child or a *marriageable* girl – more particularly, whether I am already betrothed – but, above all, whether only people of my own social standing or my social inferiors – or, what is even more important, my social superiors are in the company?

If it be true that the Baroness [von Waldstädten] herself allowed it to be done to her, the case is quite different, for she is already past her prime and cannot possibly attract any longer – and besides, she is inclined to be promiscuous with her favours. I hope, dearest friend, that even if you do not wish to become my wife, you will never lead a life like hers. If it was quite impossible for you to resist the desire to take part in the game (although it is not always wise for a man to do so, and still less for a woman), then why, in the name of Heaven did you not take the ribbon and measure your own calves *yourself* (as *all self-respecting women* have done on similar occasions in my presence) and not allow a *chapeau* [young man] to do so? – Why, I myself *in the presence of others* would never have done such a thing to you. I should have handed you the ribbon myself. Still less, then, should you have allowed it to be done to you by a stranger – a man about whom I know nothing. But it is all over now; and the least acknowledgement of your somewhat thoughtless behaviour on that occasion would have made everything all right again; and if you will not make a grievance of it, dearest friend, everything will still be all right.

You realise now how much I love you. *I do not fly into a passion as you do*. I think, I reflect and I feel. *If you will but surrender to your feelings*, then I know that this very day I shall be able to say with absolute confidence that Constanze is the virtuous, honourable, prudent and loyal sweetheart of her honest and devoted

Mozart

This surprising letter tells us quite a lot about both Mozart's and Constanze's characters, and one of their differences. While he still followed his father's standards of respectability, decorum and reserve, Constanze, no doubt dismissing the contretemps as a storm in a tea-cup, preferred a more bohemian, less pompous way of life.

The weeks were going by and there was still no sign of a softening in his father's total opposition to the marriage. A week after his protest at Constanze's behaviour, he wrote to his father asking him to ask Nannerl about the kind of fringes women were wearing in Salzburg, 'on behalf of Constanze'. He rambled on at some length, with details about Saxon piqué, satins and silks, as 'Constanze would like to send some fringes to my sister, if the latter will tell her which shade she prefers, as they are worn in all colours, white, black, green, blue, puce etc.' At the end of May Constanze wrote a second letter to Leopold Mozart, but this was, like the first, just a postscript to a letter from Wolfgang. All she said was that Wolfgang 'hasn't time to finish this letter to his dear father, which he much regrets. Please forgive me for writing to you. These few lines cannot be as agreeable to you as those which your son would have written.'

Even this brief letter was written reluctantly. 'She hesitated for some time,' Mozart told his father, 'fearing that you might laugh at her spelling and style; and she is giving me no peace until I write to you and convey her excuses.' He added a postscript himself to this letter, stating confidently that 'my dear Constanze embraces my sister as her true friend and future sister-in-law'. But still no word came from his father that he would reconcile himself to the marriage. Mozart was discovering the internal conflict which can occur when an admired parent does not approve of the object of one's affection. It is uncomfortable to look at one's fiancée through the eyes of a disapproving father, especially when up till then his judgements have been thought of as correct.

If Mozart's musical career had been as stagnant as his private life, it would have been a serious cause of disappointment. But on July 16th 1782, to the astonishment and delight of the audiences at the Burgtheater, his first full-length German opera, *The Abduction from the Seraglio*, was performed. A good description of its reception was given by the composer himself.

July 20th 1782

It was played yesterday for the second time. Can you really believe it, but yesterday there was an even stronger cabal against it than on the first evening! The whole first act was accompanied by hissing. But indeed they could not prevent the loud shouts of 'bravo' during the arias ... The theatre was almost more crowded than on the first night and on the day before the first performance no reserved seats were to be had, either in the stalls or in the third circle, and not a single box. My opera has brought in 1,200 gulden in two days. I send you herewith the original score and two copies of the libretto ... The first act, when I was sending it somewhere or other, unfortunately fell in the mud, which explains why it is so dirty.

The opera was performed sixteen times in the first couple of months, and then, in the following year was given in Prague, Mannheim, Frankfurt, Bonn and Leipzig. In 1784 it delighted audiences in Salzburg, in 1785 in Kassel, in 1787 in Breslau and Coblenz, and in 1788 in Berlin.

Mozart now was really famous, with a wide, increasingly international public. After telling his father about the opera's success, he ended the letter happily with the information that Count Zichy (whose wife was having piano lessons with Mozart) 'has this moment sent me a message inviting me to drive with him to Laxenburg, so that he may present me to Prince Kaunitz [the Emperor's chief minister]. So I must close this letter and dress.'

If only his father would change his mind about Constanze! Four days later she wrote another postscript to his sister in Salzburg, added to a brief letter from Wolfgang.

Vienna, July 24th 1782

Most precious friend,
    Forgive me for taking the liberty of worrying you again with my scrawl. Your approaching name-day must be my excuse!

And if my good wishes are a nuisance to you, as indeed all congratulations are, my consolation must be that already I am not the only one who is bothering you in this way. All that I deserve is that for the love of God you should suffer me as you do all the others. Yet could you but see into my heart and read what is there, perhaps I might be exempted from your general complaint; that at least. Possibly, no, assuredly, among the exempted I should even be given some preference. So I wish with all my heart that you will be, and not only become, very happy, and that you will really be as happy as I am confident that I shall be in the future. If you are, then...

Constanze, for some reason, stopped writing here. Leopold's and Nannerl's disapproval clearly depressed her and, no doubt, formed one of the reasons for her decision on three occasions to break off the engagement.

Rather than disappoint his father, Mozart agreed to compose a symphony without delay, although he was busy writing an arrangement of *The Abduction* for wind instruments, to prevent this being done by another hand. This new symphony (no. 35) was commissioned by Sigmund Haffner, a merchant and burgomaster of Salzburg, to celebrate the granting of a title of nobility to his son. Mozart completed this scintillating work in ten days.

All went very well at the Imperial National Theatre, where *The Abduction from the Seraglio* was being performed. 'My opera was given yesterday for the third time,' he told his father, 'and won the greatest applause; and again, in spite of the frightful heat, the theatre was packed. It was to be given next Friday, but I have protested against this, for I do not want it to become too familiar. I may say that people are absolutely infatuated with this opera. Indeed it does one good to win such approbation.' [July 27th 1782]

The same could not be said about Mozart's private life. If Frau Weber had not been making life difficult for both Mozart and Constanze, they would, no doubt, have continued to wait for Leopold's blessing. This was of cardinal importance in Wolfgang's opinion, for Leopold was not only his revered father; he was also his companion and adviser in the supremely important world of music. Their letters to each other constitute an intimate conversation on this subject. But now Mozart was finding that keeping Constanze *and* his father happy was becoming impossible. Marriage without Leopold's approval was something which Wolfgang looked on with distaste. It would be an act of betrayal, a sign that his father would justifiably regard as a rejection of his love. In making yet one more appeal for his approval, Mozart gives us a clear picture of the increasingly uncomfortable atmosphere being generated in the Weber household.

Vienna, July 27th 1782

Dearest, most beloved father,

I implore you by all you hold dear in the world to give your consent to my marriage with my dear Constanze. Do not suppose it is just for the sake of getting married. If that were the only reason, I would gladly wait. But I realise that it is absolutely necessary for my own honour and for that of my girl, and for the sake of my health and spirits. My heart is restless, and my head is confused; in such a condition how can one think and work to any good purpose? And why am I in this state? Well, because most people think that we are already married. Her mother gets very annoyed when she hears these rumours, and, as for the poor girl and myself, we are tormented to death. This state of affairs can be remedied so easily.

Believe me, it is just as easy to live in expensive Vienna as anywhere else. It all depends on economy and good management, which cannot be expected from a young fellow, particularly if he is in love. Whoever gets a wife like my Constanze will certainly be a happy man. We intend to live very modestly and quietly and yet we shall be happy. Do not be uneasy, for, if I were to fall ill to-day, which God forbid, I would wager that the leading nobles would stand by me manfully and the more so if I were married. I can say this with entire confidence. I know what Prince Kaunitz has said about me to the Emperor and to the Archduke Maximilian. Most beloved father, I am longing to have your consent. I feel sure that you will give it, for my honour and my reputation depend upon it. Do not postpone too long the joy of embracing your son and his wife. I kiss your hands a thousand times and am ever your obedient son,

W. A. Mozart

PS I embrace my dear sister most cordially. My dear Constanze sends her kind regards to you both. Adieu.

Mozart could not have made the position more clear, but four days later, having crossed with his own letter, came one from his father which indicated that even the success of *The Abduction* had failed to thaw his attitude of determined opposition. Wolfgang, it seems, was also taken to task for slighting some musicians in Salzburg. But time for Mozart was running out. He now had to tell his father that, while he and Constanze might be prepared to wait for Leopold's delayed approval, a third person, Frau Weber, was intervening and demanding that the marriage take place. A favourable reply from Leopold was wanted at once. The problem was how to make such an urgent request without making him even more adamant, even more disgusted by Frau Weber's conduct? This was Mozart's solution:

Vienna, July 31st 1782

Mon très cher Père!

I received today your letter of the 26th, a cold, indifferent letter, such as I could never have expected in reply to my news of the good reception of my opera. I thought, (judging by my own feelings) that you would hardly be able to open the parcel [containing the score] for excitement and eagerness to see your son's work, which, far from merely pleasing, is making such a sensation in Vienna that people are refusing to hear anything else, so that the theatre is always packed. It was given yesterday for the fourth time and is to be repeated on Friday. But you – have not had the time. So the whole world declares that by my boasting and criticising, I have made enemies of the professors of music and of many others! *What* world, I ask you? Presumably the world of Salzburg, for everyone in Vienna can see and hear enough to be convinced of the contrary. And that shall be my reply.

In the meantime you will have received my last letter; and I feel confident that your next letter will contain your consent to my marriage.

You can have no objection whatever to raise and indeed you do not raise any. Your letters show me that. For Constanze is a respectable, honest girl of good parentage, and I am able *to support her*. We love each other – and want each other. All that you have written, and may possibly write to me, on the subject can only be *well-meaning advice* which, however fine and good it may be, is no longer applicable to a man who has gone so far with a girl. In such a case nothing can be postponed. It is better for him to put his affairs in order and act like an honest fellow! God will ever reward that. I mean to have nothing with which to reproach myself.

Now farewell. I kiss your hands a thousand times and am ever your most obedient son

W. A. Mozart

This is an excellent letter. It is honest, persuasive and firm, without being disrespectful; the request for a reply by return of post is tactfully put. Mozart could reasonably have expected to have been granted at least a week, during which he could wait for his father's long-awaited approval. But Frau Weber was not a reasonable woman. Having persuaded Mozart to move out of her house to allay rumours about his dalliance with Constanze, a move which could be taken as confirming them, having extracted from him a marriage contract, she now threatened to call in the police.

She had made life, in one way or another, sufficiently uncomfortable for Constanze to go again to stay with Baroness von Waldstädten, who had helped Mozart with money. This escape from home provided Frau Weber with the excuse to threaten to call in the police to drag her away. Whether she agreed to let her daughter go to the Baroness in the first place or not we do not know. But now she acted, or threatened to act, as if Constanze was refusing to return. Once more Mozart gives us a close-up view of this new twist in the drama. For reasons unknown, Frau Weber was not prepared to wait for a week to hear Leopold Mozart's reply. Only two or three days after he had made his most urgent appeal for charity, Frau Weber brought matters to a head. Perhaps she was afraid that Constanze and Mozart were making love at the Baroness's house and that this was all that he had in mind.

On the 2nd (or 3rd) of August Frau Weber's maid called at Mozart's room on the third floor of no. 17, the Graben, where he had been lodging for the last nine months. She brought him some music which he had needed and asked for a written receipt, which established that he was residing at that address. She then broke the news which brought home to Mozart that Frau Weber would not be kept waiting any longer. He at once sent round a note to his friend, Baroness von Waldstädten, where Constanze was staying, asking for her advice. He must marry Constanze, he decided, at once.

[undated]

Most highly esteemed Baroness!

Madame Weber's maid has brought me my music, for which I have had to give her a receipt. She has also told me something in confidence which, although I do not believe it could happen, as it would be a disgrace to the whole family, yet seems possible when one remembers Madame Weber's stupidity, and which consequently causes me anxiety.

It appears that Sophie [the youngest daughter] went to the maid in tears. When the latter asked her what was the matter, she said: 'Do tell Mozart in secret to arrange for Constanze to go home, for my mother is absolutely determined to have her fetched by the Police.' Are the police in Vienna allowed to go into any house? Perhaps the whole thing is only a trap to make her return home.

But if it could be done, then the best plan I can think of is to marry Constanze tomorrow morning – or even to-day, if that is possible. For I should not like to expose my beloved one to this scandal – and there could not be one, if she were my wife. One thing more. Thorwart [her guardian] has been summoned to the Webers to-day. I entreat you, dear Baroness, to let me have your friendly advice and to assist us poor creatures. I shall be at home all day. I kiss your hands a thousand times and am your most grateful servant.

W. A. Mozart

In the greatest haste. Constanze knows *nothing* of this as yet. Has Herr von Thorwart been to see you? Is it necessary for the two of us to visit him after dinner today?

Mozart, it seems, was never in any doubt in his resolve to marry Constanze. But Frau Weber was not convinced. And who shall blame her? Constanze for all she knew might be pregnant. Her ruthless threat to call in the police was immediately effective. On August 4th 1782, in the cathedral of St Stephen in Vienna, Maria Constanze Weber married Wolfgang Amadeus Mozart. It was a private ceremony with only Frau Weber, her youngest daughter, Sophie, Constanze's guardian, von Thorwart, the best man, Franz von Gilovski, and a district councillor, who gave away the bride. At the conclusion of the service the bride and bridegroom could no longer remain calm and both gave way to tears. Such were the emotions of all those gathered there that all wept, Mozart has told us, 'even the priest, to see how much our hearts were moved'.

From St Stephen's the little party made their way to the house of Baroness von Waldstädten. Here they were regaled to a wedding feast which Mozart describes very briefly, but vividly, as 'more princely than baronial'. Constanze and Wolfgang must have felt most grateful to the Baroness for providing that element of warmth, fun and hospitality that had dwindled in the Weber household. In one of his jest-packed letters, in which many a true word may have been spoken, Mozart brings the thirty-three-year-old Baroness clearly before our eyes, addressing her as 'dearest, best and loveliest of all, gilt, silvered and sugared, most valued and honoured gracious Lady'. She would, we imagine, feel quite at home in *The Marriage of Figaro* or *Così fan Tutte*.

On the day after the wedding, Mozart received his father's reluctant approval.

How did all the interested parties feel, now that the wedding had at last been celebrated? Frau Weber, we can be sure, was delighted that her plain, untalented daughter, had found a husband; in fact she must have been astonished that Constanze had married a man who was indeed one in a million, a genius. Leopold Mozart, we know, was astonished, and saddened by the marriage. Mozart himself has demonstrated in all the letters that we still have, that he genuinely loved, and continued to love, his bride. As for Constanze herself, we have not a single letter to, or about Mozart, which mentions her feelings towards him. While he was alive, there is silence; after his death she remained silent. We have to form our own conclusions from the few relevant facts that can shed some light. She tore up the marriage contract that Mozart had signed. She refused him on three occasions, which shows that she was *not* certain about her own feelings towards him. And in the short postscripts that she wrote to Leopold and Nannerl, she expressed her disappointment that she was not being accepted as one of the Mozart family. Did she really love Mozart? Genius, nobility and wealth all have one quality in common. They are romantically persuasive, with a power that easily demotes physical and mental attraction from the superior position that it normally holds, when ordinary people marry. If Mozart had been a member of the aristocracy and rich, as well as being a genius and a man of great charm and vivacity, every girl in Austria would have been forgiven for marrying him in spite of her lack of real love. Mozart, when he married, was not rich, but it was clear to anyone with the least interest in music, that he possessed in abundance the ability to write music which would, given time, make money in quantity. No-one else, as far as we know, was asking Constanze to marry him, so only a fool, her mother must have told her, would throw away this extraordinary opportunity. So, when finally she found herself married to Wolfgang, the man whom her own talented sister had rejected, she no doubt resolved to do what she could to make him happy.

3

Don Giovanni
1782–88

DON OTTAVIO   Everything that pleases her gives new life to me.

DON GIOVANNI   Long live the women! Long live good wine! They sustain and glorify humanity!

DON GIOVANNI 1787

3

WHILE MOZART'S LETTERS constitute our main source of evidence of the true relationship between him and Constanze, a secondary source lies in the music which he dedicated to her. Unlike the music that he wrote for Aloysia Weber, the seven superb concert arias, mentioned in chapter 1, the works inspired by Constanze are disappointing, apart from the great *Mass in C minor*. This received its first performance in Salzburg on August 25th 1783, when Wolfgang and Constanze were staying with Leopold Mozart. For this reason there is unfortunately no letter to his father about this great occasion, when Constanze took part as one of the soprano soloists. The only comment we have from him about this Mass is in a letter to Leopold in January of that year. The wording of it is somewhat restrained:

Vienna, January 4th 1783

Mon très cher Père!

... It is quite true about my moral obligation and indeed I let the word flow from my pen on purpose. I made the promise [to bring Constanze to Salzburg] in my heart of hearts and hope to be able to keep it. When I made it, my wife was not yet married; yet, as I was absolutely determined to marry her after her recovery it was easy for me to make it – but as you yourself are aware, time and other circumstances made our journey impossible. The score of half a mass, which is still lying here waiting to be finished, is the best proof that I really made the promise.

The mass was never finished. It lacks two thirds of the Credo and all the Agnus Dei. Mozart's love of Constanze did not impel him to complete it, nor did his faith in Christianity, an emotion no doubt impaired by Archbishop Colloredo. This was his last mass, his last major religious work, apart from the uncompleted Requiem, written at the end of his life.

Four other short pieces were also dedicated to Constanze, all of them written in 1782. The first was simply a series of vocal exercises, entitled Solfeggio (K. 393).* This was followed by a sonata for violin and piano (K. 403) and an Andante and Allegretto (K. 404), also for violin and piano. Neither of these pieces was completed. Then Mozart composed a song for his wife, *In te spero* (K. 440), which is also incomplete. These light works constitute the entire musical portrait that we have of Constanze. Far greater works, far more revealing portraits, are to be found in the sublime piano concertos which Mozart dedicated to Babette Ployer (K. 449, 453, 482), Maria Theresa Paradis (K.456) and, there is reason to conclude, Magdalena Hofdemel (K. 595). All three were Mozart's piano pupils, and their musical skill was, of course, a primary motive for these dedications: but it would be short-sighted of us to ignore that, for a composer, a piano concerto is an ideal form of personal portrait, especially if it is a work in which the subject is playing the leading role.

An amusing incident occurred shortly after the wedding, when Mozart and Constanze were taking a walk in one of the parks in Vienna, the Augarten. Constanze suggested to Mozart that they should play a game with their little dog, to see what it would do if they pretended to have a fight. Constanze encouraged Wolfgang to strike her. When he did this, the Emperor happened to be passing in his carriage. He called out to them, saying 'Three weeks married and fighting already?' The newly married couple took rooms in the Wipplingerstrasse (no. 25), as neither had any intention of staying with Frau Weber. On the morning after their wedding, Anton

* This vocal exercise is named after the sol-fa syllables used since the eleventh century, when the notes of the scale were named by Guido Aretino, who was born in Paris around 995.

Stadler, the clarinettist, called on the Mozarts, but found them still asleep. Woken by his knock on the door, Wolfgang asked him in to join them at breakfast. This was cooked by Constanze, still in her wedding dress.*

To make it quite clear how happy they were together, Wolfgang, in a letter to his father, added a little couplet after his signature saying that 'Man and wife are one life.' [August 24th 1782] They could now start making plans for visits, not only to Salzburg, to see Leopold and Nannerl, but also abroad, to France and England. Without giving his own Emperor and his own country much time to acknowledge fully his powers as a composer, Mozart was already thinking he should perhaps move to another capital. He had not, of course, forgotten the acclaim that he had received in London, when only eight years old.

> The Viennese gentry, and in particular, the Emperor [he told his father] must not imagine that I am on this earth solely for the sake of Vienna. There is no monarch in the world whom I should be more glad to serve than the Emperor, but I refuse to beg for any post. I believe I am capable of doing credit to any court. If Germany, my beloved fatherland, of which, as you know, I am proud, will not accept me, then in God's name let France or England become the richer by another talented German, to the disgrace of the German nation ... Kaunitz said the other day to the Archduke Maximilian, when the conversation turned on myself, that 'such people only come into the world once in a hundred years, and must not be driven out of Germany, particularly when we are fortunate enough to have them in the capital.' ... Latterly I have been practising my French daily and have already taken three lessons in English. In three months I hope to be able to read and understand English books fairly easily.

In the following month he was ending a letter to Baroness von Waldstädten with a sentence in English: 'I kiss your hands, and hoping to see you in good health the Tuesday I am your most humble servant.'

* Ludwig Nohl, *Mozarts Leben* (Berlin, 3rd edition, 1906) p. 264.

The baroness was able to diminish, to some extent, the breach that now existed between father and son. She and Leopold exchanged letters, in which she assured him of his son's and daughter-in-law's happiness and of her continued support. His misgivings were at least partially put at rest. No doubt he was glad to have someone in Vienna with whom he could confide some of these fears, and he was most grateful to her for her invitation to stay with her when he came to Vienna – 'indeed I am quite overcome!' He was delighted, he told her, to hear that his son's wife did not take after the Webers – 'if she did, he would indeed be unhappy. Your Ladyship assures me she is a good soul – and that is enough for me!' But he still considered that Constanze was an unsuitable wife for his son. To the baroness he was openly critical of his son's character. Wolfgang was too patient, too easy-going, too proud – and too indolent. At other times he was too impatient, too hasty.

> There is either too much or too little, never the golden mean. If he is not actually in want, then he is immediately satisfied and becomes indolent and lazy. If he has to bestir himself, then he realises his worth and *wants to make his fortune at once* ... Who will prevent him from pursuing his present career in Vienna if he only has a little patience? My dear lady, please instil a little patience into my son.

Leopold was quite won over by the baroness. 'If only we were not so far from Vienna! How delightful it would be to devote ourselves together to music! May hope, sole consolation of our desires, soothe my spirit!' The baroness continued to support Wolfgang and gave him 1,000 gulden.*

A fortnight after the wedding, Mozart piously told his father that Constanze and he had often been together in church:

> even if a sense of piety had not moved us to do so, we should have had to go [on August 2nd] on account of the banns, without which we could not have been married. Indeed for a

---

* Ludwig Nohl, *Mozarts Leben*.

considerable time before we were married, we had always attended mass and gone to confession and taken communion together; and I found that I never prayed so fervently or confessed and took communion so devoutly as by her side; and she felt the same. In short, we are made for each other; and God, who orders all things and consequently had ordained this also, will not forsake us.

Leopold would have welcomed this news about their piety, but, one can be sure, he would not have agreed with his son about the Almighty's responsibility for the alliance.

Now that he was at last married to Constanze, Mozart felt that he could be more open in his comments about her mother, in his letters to his father.

I cannot understand [he said] how you got the idea that my highly honoured mother-in-law is living here too. For indeed, I did not marry my sweetheart in such a hurry in order to live a life of vexations and quarrels, but to enjoy peace and happiness; and the only way to ensure this was to cut ourselves off from that house. Since our marriage we have paid her two visits, but on the second occasion quarrelling and wrangling began again, so that my poor wife began to cry. I put a stop to the bickering at once by saying to Constanze that it was time to go. We have not been there since and do not intend to go until we have to celebrate the birthday or name-day of the mother or one of the two sisters.

In one of his letters he jokingly added a postscript, saying that Constanze was nearly ninety-one. She was, in fact, nineteen.

Even though it was written in a jesting manner, a letter of Mozart's at this time to Baroness von Waldstädten gives us perhaps some insight into his relationship with Constanze. The baroness had promised to give him a fine red coat with mother-of-pearl buttons. He wrote to thank her for her kindness, and also to put into words feelings which he could not express when he last saw her.

Vienna, October 2nd 1782

I committed a terrible blunder yesterday. I felt all the time that I had something more to say, and yet I could cudgel nothing out of my stupid skull. But it was to thank your Ladyship for having at once taken so much trouble about the beautiful coat, and for your goodness in promising to give me one like it. But it never occurred to me, which is what usually happens with me. It is my constant regret that I did not study architecture instead of music, for I have often heard it said that he is the best architect for whom nothing ever collapses. I can say with truth that I am a very happy and a very unhappy man – unhappy since the night when I saw your Ladyship at the ball with your hair so beautifully arranged – for – gone is my peace of mind! Nothing but sighs and groans! During the rest of the time I spent at the ball I did not dance – I skipped. Supper was already ordered, but I did not eat – I gobbled. During the night, instead of slumbering softly and sweetly – I slept like a dormouse and snored like a bear, and (without undue presumption) I should almost be prepared to wager that your Ladyship had the same experience *à proportion*! You smile! You blush! Ah, yes – I am indeed happy. My fortune is made!

But alas! Who taps me on the shoulder? Who peeps into my letter? Alas, alas, alas! My wife! Well, well, in the name of Heaven! I have taken her and must keep her! What is to be done? I must praise her – and imagine that what I say is true!...

But now, joking apart, if your Ladyship could send me a jugful of beer this evening, you would be doing me a great favour. For my wife is – is – is – and has longings – but only for beer prepared in the English way! Well done, little wife! I see at last that you are really good for something. My wife, who is an angel of a woman, and I, who am a model husband, both kiss your Ladyship's hands a thousand times, and are ever your faithful vassals.

In January of the new year 1783, Constanze was showing clear signs that she was pregnant. 'My little wife, who is quite plump (but only about the belly) and I both kiss your hands a thousand times and embrace our dear sister with all our hearts.' [Letter to his father, January 8th 1783] But she remained in good health, and was able to enjoy a private dance, given in their own flat, at which the men paid two gulden.

> We began at six in the evening and kept on till seven. What! Only one hour? Of course not. I meant, until seven next morning. You will wonder how I had so much room? Why, that reminds me that I have forgotten to tell you that for the last six weeks I have been living in a new lodging, only a few doors away. I have a long drawing room, a bedroom, an anteroom and a fine large kitchen. Then there are two other fine big rooms adjoining ours, which are still empty and which I used for this private ball. Baron Wetzlar and his wife were there, Baroness Waldstädten, Herr von Edelbach, that gas-bag Gilowsky, Stephanie [the librettist] and his wife, Adamberger and his wife, Lange and his [Aloysia], and so forth. It would be impossible to name them all.   [January 22nd 1783]

Another successful party was given in March, this time at a public gathering, a ridotto, or masqued ball. Mozart acted in a pantomime dressed as Harlequin, in a costume belonging to his father; his brother-in-law, Lange, was Pierrot; a dancing master, who had coached them, took the part of Pantaloon, an artist was the Doctor, and Aloysia danced and sang as Columbine. The plot and the music were composed by Mozart himself: 'I must say that we played it charmingly.' Programmes were distributed among the audience by a man in a mask, dressed as a postilion. The music for this performance (K. 446) was written for a string quartet, but only the first violin part has survived. It was at this time that Constanze's brother-in-law, Josef Lange, painted the two portraits of herself and Wolfgang. 'I think they are both good likenesses,' Mozart told his father, 'and all who have seen them are of the same opinion.'

Earlier that month Aloysia had taken the major role in a concert, the success of which Mozart must have found particularly gratifying. On March 12th 1783, he wrote:

> The theatre was very full, and I was received again by the Viennese public so cordially that I really ought to feel

delighted. I had already left the platform, but the audience would not stop clapping, and so I had to repeat the rondo for the concerto [for piano no. 5] upon which there was a regular torrent of applause ... Gluck had a box beside the Langes, in which my wife was sitting. He was loud in his praises of the symphony [no. 31], and the aria [K. 294, sung by Aloysia], and invited us all four to lunch with him next Sunday.

This triumph was followed by another splendid Mozart concert only ten days later, which he described on March 29th. 'The theatre could not have been more crowded and every box was full. But what pleased me most of all was that His Majesty the Emperor was present, and – how delighted he was and how he applauded me! His delight was beyond all bounds. He sent 25 ducats [112 gulden].' It was a long concert, consisting of Mozart's *Haffner* Symphony, of which he had already 'forgotten every single note. It positively amazed me', two of his piano concertos, four concert arias, two sets of variations for solo piano, finishing with a repeat of the last movement of the *Haffner* Symphony. This concert brought in 1,600 gulden for Mozart. Also at this time there were repeated performances of *The Abduction from the Seraglio*, 'with the usual applause from a full house'. It had been performed seventeen times in the first six months. As W. J. Turner points out in his biography of Mozart, 'it is clear that he earned a considerable amount of money in Vienna during these years.'

Leopold Mozart's pessimistic forecasts of misery and neglect were proving false. He must have been cheered also to hear that Wolfgang and Constanze were happy together. In May, they spent the day together out of doors in the Prater.

I simply cannot make up my mind to drive back into town so early. The weather is far too lovely and it is far too delightful in the Prater today. We have taken our lunch in the fresh air and shall stay on until eight or nine in the evening. My whole company consists of my little wife who is pregnant, and hers consists of her little husband, who is not pregnant, but fat and flourishing. I must ask you to wait patiently for a longer letter and the aria and variations – for, of course, I cannot finish them in the Prater; and for the sake of my dear little wife I cannot miss this fine weather. Exercise is good for her.   [May 3rd 1783]

Six weeks later, on June 17th, Constanze gave birth to her first child, Raimund Leopold, a 'fine sturdy boy, as round as a ball'. Her pregnancy had also achieved an improvement in her relationship with her mother. 'My mother-in-law,' wrote Wolfgang, 'by her great kindness to her daughter has made full amends for all the harm she did her *before her marriage*. She spends the whole day with her.' Even this important event did not produce, as far as we know, a letter from Constanze herself, but Mozart has given us more details about the early days of his first-born than any other famous composer whose letters have been preserved.

Vienna, June 18th 1783

Her pains began at half past one in the morning, so that night we both lost our rest and sleep. At four o'clock I sent for my mother-in-law – and then for the midwife. At six o'clock the child began to appear and at half past six the trouble was all over. My dear wife is as well as she can be in the circumstances. I trust with God's help that, as she is taking good care of herself, she will make a complete recovery from her confinement. From the condition of her breasts I am rather afraid of milk-fever. And now the child has been given to a foster nurse against my will, or rather, at my wish! For I was quite determined that, whether she should be able to do so or not, my wife was never to feed her child. Yet I was quite determined that my child was never to take the milk of a stranger. I wanted the child to be brought up on water, like my sister and myself. However the midwife, my mother-in-law and most people here have begged and implored me not to allow it, if only for the reason that most children here who are brought up on water do not survive, as the people here do not know how to do it properly. That induced me to give in, for I should not like to have anything to reproach myself with.

After my wife's safe delivery, I immediately sent a message to Baron Raimund Wetzlar, who is a good and true friend of mine. He came to see us at once and offered to stand godfather ... He said very cheerfully: 'Ah, now you have a little Raimund,' and kissed the child.

[June 21st 1783] Thank God, my wife has now survived the two critical days, yesterday and the day before, and in the circumstances is very well. We now hope that all will go well. The child too is quite strong and healthy, and has a tremendous number of things to do, I mean, drinking, sleeping, yelling, pissing, shitting, dribbling and so forth. He kisses the hands of his grandpapa and of his aunt. Herr von Gilowsky sends his greetings to both of you, and thanks to his father and to others for never writing to him – although they must know that he is laid up with a fever.

The last movement of Mozart's beautiful string quartet, in D minor (K. 421), was written during the night of the 16th, when Constanze was hourly waiting for the birth of her child. As Sacheverall Sitwell has written in his biography of Mozart, it is one of the loveliest pieces of music he ever wrote.

With the successful arrival of Mozart's son and heir, plans could be made for a visit to Salzburg; Leopold could meet Constanze and perhaps he might change his mind about her. She was still not certain that this was possible. With surprising candour, Mozart indicated to his father that she was reluctant to make this journey (July 12th 1783). 'She is a little bit nervous lest you should not like her, because she is not pretty. But I console her as well as I can by telling her that my dearest father thinks more of inward than of outward beauty.' There was also another problem. Some of Mozart's friends had suggested to him that he might be arrested in Salzburg, as he had never received a formal notice of dismissal from the Archbishop. 'Perhaps he has purposely held it back, in order to catch me later. If you agree with me [that arrest is possible] then we must arrange another place for our meeting – perhaps Munich. For a priest is capable of anything.'

Such a suggestion, thought Leopold, was sheer humbug,

merely a way of saying that Wolfgang did not really want to see him again. Wolfgang was delighted to hear that he need not fear arrest in Salzburg and assured his father that he really did look forward to seeing him again. On July 12th, he wrote:

> You have now set my mind completely at rest, and we shall come in August, or certainly September at the latest. Have I ever given you the impression that I had no desire or longing to see you? Most certainly never! If you insist on calling what are real obstacles mere humbug, I cannot prevent you from doing so. But assuredly you will have observed that I have no desire whatever to see Salzburg or the Archbishop. I care very little for Salzburg and nothing at all for the Archbishop; I shit on both of them. It would never enter my head voluntarily to make a journey thither, were it not that you and my sister lived there. I must close, as I have a good deal to write. Meanwhile, arrange the bowling-green in the garden, for my wife is a great lover of the game.

Leopold's confidence in his son's safety in Salzburg could not, however, overcome Wolfgang's misgivings.

> Many people here are alarming me to such an extent that I cannot describe it. However much I protest, I am told: *'Well, you will see; you will never get away again. You have no idea what that wicked, malevolent Prince* [the Archbishop] *is capable of! And you cannot conceive what low tricks are resorted to in affairs of this kind. Take my advice and meet your father in some third place.'* As far as I am concerned, whatever happened would not worry me very much, for I can now adapt myself to any circumstances. But when I think of my wife and my little Raimund, then my indifference ceases.'

But, Leopold was told, the Archbishop's reassurance was enough.

Wolfgang and Constanze were delighted with their child, who looked just like his father. 'It is just as if my face had been copied.' Mozart stressed that they were looking forward to seeing Leopold and Nannerl, and added that he had a plan for meeting somewhere else, if, after all, Leopold changed his mind. This remark was followed by a little excursion into philosophy which perhaps gives us an indication that Mozart was not completely happy. 'I am convinced that if one is to enjoy a great pleasure, one must forgo something. Why! In the greatest happiness there is always something lacking.'

Constanze hardly ever put pen to paper, but in July of this year, 1783 she wrote two short letters, one to Nannerl, Wolfgang's sister, the other to Margarete Marchand, a friend who was staying with the Mozarts and who was being given singing lessons by Leopold.

Vienna, July 19th 1783

Most precious and dearest Mademoiselle Sister-in-law!

My dear husband has received your letter and both he and I are delighted that you are looking forward so much to seeing us. But he was a little annoyed by your suspicion that we were not so very anxious to see you; and indeed I myself felt rather hurt. To prove that everything is all right again, let me tell you that we always intended to go to you in August; and so we wanted to give you a little surprise, which will no longer be one for you, but will be so at any rate for our dear beloved father – that is, if you can keep it quiet, which we beg you to do; for only on this condition are we telling you the truth. Well, you have dragged our secret out of us by your naughty letter; and we shall be quite content if only we give this unexpected pleasure to our dear father. So – please do not mention our plan. Well, about August 1st I shall have the joy and happiness of embracing you. Until then I remain with the deepest respect, my dearest sister-in-law, yours sincerely

Maria Constanza Mozart

Vienna, July 19th 1783

Dearest Mademoiselle Marchand!

I am delighted that you still remember me and have taken the trouble to write to me. Believe me, I am just as much longing to see Salzburg and have the joy and happiness of meeting

personally my dear papa-in-law and my dear sister-in-law and
showing them my devotion as you can possibly be longing
for an opportunity of seeing your own beloved parents again.
And then the pleasure of embracing my dear Mademoiselle
Marguerite, whom I knew in Mannheim and Munich as a very
clever young woman and who in the meantime has had plenty
of opportunity of perfecting her gifts! How delighted I shall be
to see her again, kiss her and admire her talents. God willing, I
shall be able to do so on August 1st. Meanwhile I urge you to
observe the strictest silence and I remain your most devoted
servant and friend

Maria Constanza Mozart

At the end of July Constanze and Wolfgang journeyed to
Salzburg for a three-month stay with Leopold and Nannerl,
leaving behind their six-weeks-old baby, Raimund. We do not
know with whom he was left. Staying with Leopold was
Margarete Marchand and her brother, who was learning to
play the violin. The visit did not achieve any real rapprochement between Leopold and Constanze, for the simple reason
that meeting her only confirmed what Leopold had thought all
along. If he had written to his son and had said anything that
was complimentary, after the visit, there would have been no
reason for Constanze to destroy the letter, as she did with the
rest of his correspondence after her marriage.

We have no letters from Mozart which tell us anything
about the visit, only the entries in Nannerl's diary, which tell
us little. The weather was good for most of the time, but in
October it was misty. The family enjoyed musical parties in
the house and visits from other musicians. They went for
walks into the country; Constanze is occasionally mentioned
briefly as 'my sister-in-law', without any further comment.
On the last Sunday of their stay, they all went to St Peter's
Church in Salzburg for the first performance of Mozart's *Mass
in C minor* (K. 427), with Constanze and, possibly, Margarete
singing the two soprano solo parts. How well they sang, how
successfully the choir and the orchestra performed this work,
the finest of his fourteen masses, we do not know. In a long

letter written to his father from Linz, where he and Constanze went on leaving Salzburg, he thanked him, saying, 'my wife and I kiss your hands, ask you to forgive us for inconveniencing you for so long and thank you once more very much for all the received –' The word left out was perhaps 'kindnesses'. He had just told his father that in four days' time he was taking part in a concert in Linz, and that, as he had no score of any of his symphonies with him, he was writing a new one 'at break-neck speed'.

No symphony could be more serene; no work conceals so successfully its rapid composition. The *Linz* (no. 36) radiates a feeling of happiness and perhaps relief that the visit to Salzburg had been comparatively successful. Now that his father had at last met Constanze, he could look forward to welcoming his father in his own home in Vienna. In Linz he and Constanze were the guests of Count Johann Joseph Thun-Hohenstein. On arrival at the city gates, they were met by one of the Count's servants, and they were then driven to the family mansion. 'I really cannot tell you what kindnesses the family are showering upon us,' wrote Mozart a few days before the concert. When Mozart was only six, in 1762, twenty-one years earlier, he had given a little recital in an inn here in Linz. This was his first public performance. His present stay in this town, probably for a fortnight, was, we can assume, one of the happiest occasions of his life.

Constanze and Wolfgang arrived back in Vienna in early December – to find that their son was dead. We do not know the cause of his death or how they both reacted. In the following month Constanze again was pregnant and gave birth to another son, Karl Thomas, on September 21st 1784. He lived until 1859.

This year, 1784, in which Constanze gave birth to her second son, saw also the composition of six piano concertos, nos. 14–19, and in the autumn Wolfgang began his magnificent opera, *The Marriage of Figaro*. It was for the Mozarts an *annus mirabilis*.

Four of these concertos were specially written for people he knew and admired. One of them, no. 19 (K. 459) was dedicated to Prince Joseph von Furstenberg; the others were dedicated to his piano pupils, Barbara Ployer and Maria Theresa Paradis. Most of Mozart's pupils were young women; of the sixteen pupils to whom he is known to have given lessons, thirteen were women.* Barbara Ployer was the daughter of Gottfried Ignaz von Ployer, the Agent of the Salzburg Court in Vienna. Inspired by her, Mozart wrote the first and fourth of the 1784 concertos, nos. 14 (K. 449) and 17 (K. 453), and another piano concerto, no. 22 (K. 482) in the following year. He also gave her lessons in composition. For these concertos Mozart tells us, she 'paid me handsomely'. The other concerto, written in 1784 for a special person, was no. 18 (K. 456), which he composed for Maria Theresa von Paradis, a Viennese pianist who was blind. In 1784 she made a successful tour of the major European capitals; Haydn was so impressed by her skill that he dedicated his Concerto in G to her. In February of the following year Mozart played the concerto written for her in Vienna. Leopold Mozart was there: 'I was sitting only two boxes away from the very beautiful Princess of Württemberg,' he told Nannerl, 'and had the great pleasure of hearing so clearly all the interplay of the instruments that for sheer delight tears came into my eyes. When your brother left the platform the Emperor waved his hat and called out "Bravo, Mozart!" And when he came on to play, there was a great deal of clapping.' [February 14th 1785] Two other beautiful pieces were written for a pupil at this time. The Piano Sonata in C minor (K. 457) and the Fantasia for piano, in the same key (K. 475) were composed for Therese, the wife of Johann von Trattner, a printer and bookseller, into whose house in Vienna Mozart and Constanze moved in January of this year. On at least two occasions Wolfgang wrote to Therese, but these letters have

---

* Rosa Cannabich, Therese Pierron Serrarius, Countess Marie von Rumbeck, Josephine Auernhammer, Therese von Trattner, Countess Wilhelmine von Thun, Countess Anna Maria von Zichy, Countess Josepha Gabriele Palfy, Barbara Ployer, Franziska von Jacquin, Caroline Pichler, Magdalena Hofdemel, Maria Theresa Paradis.

not been traced.* At a concert given in Trattner's house, Mozart made more than 550 gulden.

One of Mozart's biographers, Michael Levey, has, with some justification, declared that 'in his imagination, Mozart was something of a Don Giovanni'. According to Jacob Henickstein, whose sister was given a few lessons by Mozart, he was always in love with his pupils. This remark, made to Vincent and Mary Novello in 1829, may have been a hint that one of these women was indeed loved by him.† We know that one of them, Josephine Auernhammer, was for a time in love with Mozart, but he did not find her physically attractive.‡ He arranged for her to live with Baroness von Waldstädten, when she became a professional pianist, and he dedicated six violin and piano sonatas to her (K. 296, 376–380). In 1796 she married a certain Herr Bösenhönig. There is no evidence that he fell in love with any of the other pupils to whom he openly dedicated his work. Such dedications were a public recognition of his admiration of their talents as musicians, but he has left no acknowledgement that he was in love with any of them. However, he may well have found them attractive. The woman who was thus acknowledged publicly, who inspired the greatest of Mozart's dedicated works, the 14th, 17th and 22nd Piano Concertos, Barbara, or Babette, Ployer, married, some time before 1800, Herr Bojanovich, the son of the Hungarian ambassador in Vienna.

If Mozart fell in love with one of his other piano pupils, it would naturally be an occasion for silence on his part, and, if he did express his love for her in a letter, we can be quite certain that Constanze would wish to destroy it. If he composed a piano concerto for a pupil with whom he was in love, he would conceal the fact that she had inspired the work. Such a concerto would, it might be expected, have something in common with the concertos written for Babette Ployer. It

* G. Nottebohm, *Mozartiana*, (Leipzig, 1880), p. 131.
† *A Mozart Pilgrimage*, ed. Rosemary Hughes, Novello 1955, p. 159.
‡ Letter to his father, August 22nd 1781.

would be a work full of joy and tenderness, with elements of intimacy and reserve.

1784 was also a good year for Nannerl Mozart. On August 23rd she married Johann Baptist von Berchtold zu Sonnenburg, the magistrate of St Gilgen, where her mother was born, eighteen miles from Salzburg. He was a widower, with five children. Leopold Mozart was now left alone. Thinking that he would prefer to live with his daughter or his son, Wolfgang suggested that he should terminate his service with the Archbishop and move to St Gilgen or Vienna. But he preferred to go on living in Salzburg, paying just one visit to Wolfgang and Constanze in 1785.

Writing to congratulate Nannerl on her good fortune, Mozart wrote her an amusing nuptial ode, the last two lines of which may have been taken from a book of English verse, first published in 1707, Playford's *Wit and Mirth*.

> Wedlock will show you many things
> Which still a mystery remain.
> Experience soon will teach to you
> What Eve herself once had to do
> Before she could give birth to Cain.
> But all these duties are so light
> You will perform them with delight.
> Yet no state is an unmixed joy,
> And marriage has its own alloy,
> Lest us its bliss perhaps should cloy.
> So when your husband shows reserve,
> Or wrath which you do not deserve,
> And perhaps a nasty temper too,
> Think, sister, 'tis a man's queer way,
> Say: 'Lord, thy will be done by day,
> But mine at night you'll do.'

Mozart told Nannerl that he hoped she and her husband would live together as harmoniously as he and Constanze did.

In February of the following year, 1785, Leopold was able to see for himself how well his son and Constanze were getting on together. His letters from Vienna to Nannerl describing his visit must have cheered her considerably.

Vienna, February 14th 1785

That your brother has very fine quarters with all the necessary furniture you may gather from the fact that his rent is 460 gulden. On the same evening that we arrived we drove to his first subscription concert, at which a great many members of the aristocracy were present. Each person pays a souverain d'or or three ducats [13 gulden] for these Lent concerts. Your brother is giving them at the Mehlgrube and only pays half a souverain d'or each time for the hall. The concert was magnificent and the orchestra played magnificently. We had a new and very fine [clavier] concerto by Wolfgang, which the copyist was still copying when we arrived [no. 21].

On Saturday evening Herr Joseph Haydn came to see us and the three new quartets were performed.* Haydn said to me, 'Before God and as an honest man I tell you that your son is the greatest composer known to me, either in person or by name. He has taste and, what is more, the most profound knowledge of composition.' Little Karl [Wolfgang's son, now five months old] is the picture of him. He seems very healthy. He is extremely friendly and laughs when spoken to. I have only seen him cry once and the next moment he started to laugh.

February 21st 1785

We lunched on Thursday with your brother's mother-in-law, Frau Weber. I must tell you that the meal, which was neither too lavish nor too stingy, was cooked to perfection. The roast was a fine plump pheasant; and everything was excellently well prepared.

March 12th 1785

Your brother made 559 gulden at his concert. He has also been playing frequently at other concerts in the theatre ... We never get to bed before one o'clock, and I never get up before nine. We lunch at two or half past. Every day there are concerts; and

---

* K. 458, 464, 465. For the six quartets dedicated to Haydn, Mozart was paid 500 gulden.

the whole time is given up to teaching, music, composing and so forth. It is impossible for me to describe the rush and bustle. Since my arrival your brother's forte piano has been taken at least a dozen times to the theatre or some other house.

March 19th 1785

If my son has no debts to pay, I think he can now lodge two thousand gulden in the bank. Certainly the money is there, and so far as eating and drinking is concerned, the housekeeping is extremely economical.

Leopold visited Constanze's sister, Aloysia and heard her sing some arias, finding her voice too loud for a small audience in a drawing-room, but he was pleased when she sang quietly. Josef Lange, her husband, impressed him with a sketch of himself, which has not been traced. The year before, Wolfgang had become a Mason. Leopold now joined the same lodge, and, pleased to be able to make this significant sign of *rapprochement*, returned to Salzburg. Another happy event during his stay was a visit to Baroness von Waldstädten, who was then living just outside Vienna. Leopold had been looking forward to meeting 'this woman of my heart, since I, unseen, have been the man of her heart'.

What Leopold really thought now about Constanze we do not know, but he must have been delighted by his son's success in Vienna, both as a composer and as a pianist. He had, in fact, been so successful that in 1786 he began to make plans for a return visit to England, where he had scored such a triumph back in 1764, when he was eight years old. This might well have taken place if Leopold had agreed to look after Mozart's little son, Karl, and a second baby, Johann, who had been born on October 18th 1786. But Leopold was already looking after Nannerl's baby, who had entered on the scene in June of the year before.

This piece of family information had not been passed on to Constanze and Wolfgang; they had heard it from a mutual friend in Vienna. And Leopold was unwilling to help with yet another child: 'They could go off and travel – they might even die – or remain in England – and I should have to run off after them with the children. As for the payment which he offers me for the children and for maids to look after them, well – Basta! He will find my excuse very clear and instructive.' In spite of this discouragement, Mozart was still thinking of going to England in January of the new year 1787, telling a friend, Baron Gottfried von Jacquin, that he might soon have to forgo the pleasure of seeing him and his family for a long time, perhaps for ever. On April 24th 1787, Wolfgang wrote in the album of the baron's sister, Franziska, one of his piano pupils, in English: 'Don't never forget your true and faithful friend.'

But even if Leopold had agreed to look after Constanze's children, it is possible that Wolfgang would have stayed in Vienna, as he was constantly in demand, too busy, it seems, to let his father know that his third child, Johann Thomas Leopold, died after less than a month, in November 1786. Neither he nor Constanze told Leopold about this; he learnt the news from some English friends he and his son had made in Salzburg and Vienna – Nancy Storace, an excellent singer, her brother, Stephen, who had composed two operas, and had been given some lessons in compositions by Wolfgang, Thomas Attwood, also a composer and pupil of Mozart, and Michael Kelly, a first-class singer from Dublin, who had trained in Naples. The Prince who had commissioned Mozart to write a piano concerto two years before, in 1784, Joseph von Furstenberg, now asked him to compose another concerto (no. 23, K. 488) and also to send him the score of three symphonies he had already written. These five works, together with the score of another of the great 1784 piano concertos (no. 16) brought a payment of 143½ gulden from the Prince. Earlier in this busy year, on May 1st, the curtain went up for the first performance of *The Marriage of Figaro*, with Nancy Storace as Susanna and Michael Kelly as Basilio and Don Curzio.

Mozart wrote a concert aria specially for Nancy Storace (K. 505) towards the end of 1786; he recorded the composition of it in his notebook as written 'for Mad.selle Storace and me'. It is indeed a superb tribute and it can be described as a love letter in music. Nancy now returned to England and never came back to Vienna.

In April 1786 Leopold Mozart had written to his daughter, Nannerl, with news about the forthcoming production of *The Marriage of Figaro*:

> The opera is being performed for the first time [on May 1st]. It will be surprising if it is a success, for I know that very powerful cabals have ranged themselves against your brother. Salieri [the Court *Kappellmeister*] and his supporters will try to move heaven and earth to down his opera. Duschek [a Czech composer] told me recently that it is on account of the very great reputation which your brother's exceptional talent and ability have won for him that so many people are plotting against him.

In spite of Salieri and his supporters, *The Marriage of Figaro* was a success right from the start. There was much applause and many encores at the first night. There was some hissing from people in the top gallery, but their opposition was completely ineffective. It continued to be well received in Vienna and in Prague, where it was produced in the same year.

Mozart and Constanze were invited to Prague and arrived on January 11th 1787, and a special poem was composed in his honour. As Michael Levey says in his biography of Mozart, this opera is 'the marriage of so much. Ultimately it is a marriage of words and music which makes it probably the most perfect of all operas. Mozart was no doubt inspired by the vision of an ideal world where men may meet as equals, rewarded by love from women who are also at least their equal. A marriage of love is meant to be a marriage of true minds as well.' Mozart himself has described, in a letter to his friend, Baron Gottfried von Jacquin, how the men and women of Prague took to his new opera:

Prague, January 14th 1787

At six o'clock I drove with Count Canal [von Malabaila] to the Bretfeld ball, where the cream of the beauties of Prague usually gather. Why – *you* ought to have been there, my friend! I fancy I see you running after all those pretty women, married and unmarried! I neither danced nor flirted with any of them, the former, because I was too tired, and the latter owing to my natural bashfulness. I looked on, however, with the greatest pleasure while all these people flew about in sheer delight to the music of my *Figaro*, arranged for quadrilles and waltzes. For here they talk about nothing but *Figaro*. Nothing is played, sung or whistled but *Figaro*. No opera is drawing like *Figaro*. Nothing, nothing but *Figaro*. Certainly a great honour for me!

In February 1787, Mozart and Constanze returned to Vienna, the richer by 1,000 gulden, good news which Leopold learnt from the English party, the Storaces, Kelly and Attwood, when they visited him in Salzburg. This year was also a year of masterpieces, including the popular *Eine kleine Nachtmusik*, three superb string quintets (K. 406, 515, 516), and *Don Giovanni*. In April of this successful year Ludwig van Beethoven, now sixteen years old, came to Vienna for a brief fortnight's stay. He certainly would have stayed longer if it had not been for his mother's ill health and approaching death. He came to Mozart, the most famous composer in the country, for a few lessons, and impressed Wolfgang so much that he said to some friends, who were sitting in an adjoining room during the first meeting, 'Keep your eyes on him; some day he will give the world something to talk about.'

But in April a dear friend, Count August von Hatzfeld, a gifted violinist, died, and, in the following month, Leopold Mozart. How Wolfgang reacted can be inferred from a letter which he wrote to his father at the beginning of April, and also from *Don Giovanni*, which he was composing at this time. His letter to his father is as profound as the two letters he wrote at the time of his mother's death in Paris nine years earlier:

Vienna, April 4th 1787

I hear that you are really ill. I need hardly tell you how greatly I am longing to receive some reassuring news from yourself.

And I still expect it, although I have now made a habit of being prepared in all affairs of life for the worst. As death, when we come to consider it closely, is the true goal of our existence, I have formed during the last few years such close relations with this best and truest friend of mankind that his image is not only no longer terrifying to me, but is indeed very soothing and consoling! And I thank my God for graciously granting me the opportunity of learning that death is the *key* which unlocks the door to our true happiness. I never lie down at night without reflecting that – young as I am – I may not live to see another day. Yet no-one of all my acquaintances could say that in company I am morose or disgruntled. For this blessing I daily thank my Creator and wish with all my heart that each one of my fellow creatures could enjoy it.

In the letter which Madame Storace took away with her [addressed to Leopold], I expressed my views to you on this point, in connection with the sad death of my dearest and most beloved friend, Count von Hatzfeld. He was just thirty-one, my age. I do not feel sorry for him, but I pity most sincerely both myself and all who knew him as well as I did.

I hope and trust that while I am writing this, you are feeling better. But, if contrary to all expectation, you are not recovering, I implore you not to hide it from me, but to tell me the whole truth, or get someone to write it to me, so that as quickly as is humanly possible I may come to your arms. I entreat you by all that is sacred – to both of us.

Leopold died eight weeks later on May 28th 1787. In *Don Giovanni* Mozart expressed emotions which were no doubt his own in regard to his now dead father. Don Giovanni kills Donna Anna's father, who later returns from the dead to punish him for his conduct. The stage father figure, who returns to life in the form of a statue, or ghost, can be seen as Wolfgang's own father, a man who created him physically as a man and professionally as a composer. Mozart knew that his father was bitterly disappointed by his marriage, by his egoistic revolt against his holy employer in Salzburg, by his general attitude of intellectual independence and by the fact that he still had no official appointment. Wolfgang was always

aware of the debt he owed to his father; Leopold, a cautious
and deferential man, was always aware, and perhaps resentful,
of his son's attitude of masterly self-confidence.

On the death of Leopold, Wolfgang and Nannerl received in
his will 1,000 gulden each. In September he and Constanze
went to Prague, for the first performance of *Don Giovanni*, for
which he was paid 900 gulden. The opera was first performed
on October 29th 1787, and 'it was received with the greatest
applause. It was performed yesterday for the fourth time, for
my benefit. People here are doing their best to persuade me to
remain for a couple of months and write another opera. But I
cannot accept this proposal, however flattering it may be.'
[Letter to Baron von Jacquin, November 3rd 1787]

Returning to Vienna, Wolfgang and Constanze were
greeted by more good news. On December 7th 1787, Mozart
was rewarded by an appointment as *Kammerkomponist* to the
Emperor, Joseph II, with an annual income of 800 gulden. 'I
am sure you will be pleased to hear it,' he wrote to Nannerl. He
knew that their father would have been thrilled. 'I have now a
permanent appointment, but *for the time being* at a salary of only
800 gulden. However, no-one else in the household is drawing
so large a sum.' [Letter to his sister, August 2nd 1788] His
predecessor, Gluck, who had died in November 1787, had
been paid 2,000 gulden, so Mozart could in time expect a
similar amount. Mozart's salary was twice that of Joseph
Haydn, the *Kapellmeister* to Prince Nikolaus Esterhazy.

Soon after the great success of *Don Giovanni* and the royal
appointment, Constanze gave birth to a daughter on
December 27th 1787. Her son Karl was now three years old.
There is no evidence that either she or Wolfgang wanted many
children, so they may well have felt that they now had a
complete family. In the following year, 1788, Mozart created
some of his most sublime compositions, the Piano Concerto,
no. 26, in D major (K. 537), and the three majestic symphonies,
nos. 39, 40 and 41. All these works are radiant, joyful, electrify-
ing and full of confidence.

Several times a year in his house in Prague, Franz Roth, the official accommodation supervisor of the town, held concerts and recitals. He asked Haydn if he could compose a comic opera. Haydn declined the invitation, saying that 'all my operas are far too closely connected with our personal circle [at Esterhaza, in Hungary], and moreover they would not produce the proper effect.' He went on to recommend his friend Mozart, saying that if he did write an opera for Prague, he would 'be risking a good deal, for scarcely any man can brook comparison with the great Mozart.'

> If I could only impress on the soul of every friend of music, and on important persons in particular, how inimitable are Mozart's works, how profound, how musically intelligent, how extraordinarily sensitive! – why then the nations would vie with each other to possess such a jewel within their frontiers. Prague should hold him fast – but should reward him too; for without this, the history of great geniuses is sad indeed, and gives but little encouragement to posterity to further exertions; and unfortunately this is why so many promising intellects fall by the wayside. It enrages me to think that this incomparable Mozart is not yet engaged by some imperial or royal court! Forgive me if I lose my head: but I love the man so dearly. [December 1787]*

It is at this stage in the story of Mozart, that paradox begins to dominate. Our supply of letters from Mozart, till now our prime source of evidence, declines sadly, and what we do have often refer to the subject of Mozart's borrowing of money from his friend and fellow Mason, Michael Puchberg. Here lies the paradox. Mozart's biographers agree that during the first four years of his marriage, when he had no official position or salary, his talent as composer and pianist brought him sufficient funds. We know that Mozart earned a considerable amount of money during these years. Now, when the public flocked to his operas, and the Emperor gave him regular employment, Mozart had to borrow money from a friend on

* *The Collected Correspondence of Joseph Haydn*, ed. H. C. Robbins Landon, (Barrie and Rockliff, 1959) p. 73.

fifteen occasions. Expenses for his wife and family could not have been great, as after only six months, their daughter, Therese, died, on June 29th 1788. There is no evidence that either Constanze or Wolfgang was extravagant or uneconomical. In May of this year *Don Giovanni* was performed in Vienna, but we have no letter from him about this great event. He was paid 225 gulden, but this was not enough to make a loan unnecessary. Of all Mozart's biographers, only Sacheverell Sitwell honestly admits that here we are truly confronted by a mystery. Was there, he asks, a secret cause for this need for more money, of which we are ignorant? The answer is clearly that we are ignorant of the true state of Mozart's financial position at this time, and of the real nature of his relationship with Constanze. The sudden paucity of Mozart's letters written in the last three years of his life indicates that many may have been destroyed by Constanze. The only reasons put forward by historians for this need for more money relate to overwork, lack of recognition and the state of Constanze's health.

The first two suggested causes of poverty are without foundation. Mozart was not overworked, and he was now a celebrity. His marriage appeared happy enough. In August 1788, a party of Danish actors visited the Mozarts, when they were living in the suburbs of Vienna. Their young boy, Karl, sang some songs in the garden; Constanze cut some quills which the copyist would need, and Wolfgang extemporised happily on the piano. In the previous two months his friend Puchberg had lent him money to settle his account with his former landlord and to raise some money on two pawnbroker tickets. But Constanze was beginning to suffer from ill-health. In the following summer she went to stay at the health resort at Baden, seventeen miles from Vienna. How necessary this and other visits to this place in 1790 and 1791 were we do not know. We do not know the exact nature of Constanze's illness. Her foot was the main trouble, and in one letter to Puchberg Mozart wrote that *'if she had not contracted bed-sores*, which make her condition most wretched, she would be able to sleep. The only fear is that the bone may be affected.' We have no further information about her health for the rest of her long life. She died at the age of seventy-nine.

Mozart borrowed money from Puchberg for Constanze's stay at Baden on perhaps several occasions; but one letter from Mozart, written in June 1791, indicates that, by this time at any rate, he was not worried about these costs.

To Choir-master Stoll at Baden. June 1791

Will you please find a small apartment for my wife? She needs only two rooms, or one room and a dressing-room. But the main thing is that they should be on the ground floor. The rooms which I should prefer are those which Goldhahn used to occupy on the ground floor at the butcher's. Please enquire there first; perhaps they are still to let. My wife is going out to Baden on Saturday, or Monday at the latest. If we cannot have these rooms, then you must look for something fairly near the baths. The ground floor at the town notary's, where Dr Alt stayed, would do very well.

This is not the letter of a man in dire financial straits. Constanze stayed here for extended periods in 1789, '90 and '91.

In 1788 we have only five letters written by Mozart – one to his sister, asking her to send him some music by Michael Haydn, Joseph's brother, who was living in Salzburg, and four to Puchberg, each one a request for a loan. Most of these requests were granted without delay. The first letter that we have for the following year, 1789, written at the end of March, is also a request for a loan, for 100 gulden. It was written to another fellow Mason, Franz Hofdemel, whose beautiful wife, Magdalena, was a gifted pianist and a pupil of Mozart's.

4

Così fan tutte
or
In love with two women
1789–91

DON ALFONSO	The more sighs and tears, the more ready women become for a change of lovers.
FERRANDO	When the heart is nourished with hope and love, no other joy is needed.
DESPINA	Never reject the chance to have some fun! You must now learn to have your cake and eat it. We women have so little chance to amuse ourselves, that we must take it as it comes.
FIORDILIGI AND FERRANDO	Kiss me, my darling, and let sweet affection and sighs of pleasure comfort us for so much suffering and pain!

COSÌ FAN TUTTE *1790*

4

1789 IS THE ONLY YEAR in the last fifteen years of Mozart's life
in which he wrote no symphony or concerto. We only have
sixteen of his letters for this year; most of them are short letters
to his wife, written when he was away from Vienna or when
she was staying in Baden for her health. The diminished
output of work and the anxieties expressed in the letters have
led Mozart's biographers, worried by the approaching
ignominious burial of the composer, to start looking for
tragedies in his life which could account for this shameful end.
This insistence on the tragic is in fact wisdom after the event.
On examination of the evidence available we can see that it
lacks conviction. A good example of the commiseration that
historians have bestowed on Mozart at this time appears in
Michael Levey's biography: 'It was in this very period of
experiences blacker than any he had known before, and without any likelihood of things improving, that Mozart created
his three famous last symphonies, finished within six weeks of
each other.' To prepare the reader for Mozart's burial in an
unmarked grave, to minimise the shock of this surprising
treatment, historians have painted a picture in which misery,
torment and an element of failure dominate the foreground.

What have we, in fact, to go on, to form a true picture of
these last four years of Mozart's life? He wrote less music in
1788 and 1789, but that is no proof of misery. It could, on the
contrary, indicate that he was spending more time enjoying
himself. The music itself can be examined for signs of storm
and stress; but this is a dangerous practice. It can lead one to
pounce on any theme or chord that is not happy or tranquil,

and ignore or explain away more frequent elements that do indicate these qualities. The same double standard can be used when reading Mozart's letters, with the suggestion that when Mozart was being cheerful he was merely masking his grief.

In his letters, it is true, Mozart reveals two serious causes of anxiety, lack of money and his wife's behaviour at Baden. 'I am glad when you have some fun [at Baden] – of course I am,' he wrote to Constanze in August 1789, 'but I do wish that you would not sometimes make yourself so cheap. You are too free and easy with ... [the name has been deleted] And it was the same with ... when he was still at Baden. Remember that you yourself once admitted to me that you were inclined to *comply too easily*.' In the same letter Mozart told Constanze that she should not torment herself or him 'with unnecessary jealousy'.

So Constanze was being 'free and easy' with another man at this time, and Mozart was making her jealous by his friendship with another woman. Discovering who these two people were may not be very difficult. The cause of Mozart's need for more money presents greater problems. In a letter to Michael Puchberg, written in March 1790, he urgently appealed for another loan. His friend agreed and sent him 150 gulden. In making this request Mozart wrote: 'You know how my present circumstances, were they to become known, would damage the chances of my application to the Court, and how necessary it is that they should remain a secret.' Mozart was applying for promotion to the rank of *Kapellmeister*.

Here, in one letter, Mozart mentions both his need of money and the necessity of secrecy, lest his present circumstances should become known. We have no letters from Puchberg to help us and what we know about him gives us no clue. He was a wealthy merchant of Vienna; his family had become prosperous as wine merchants, and he had joined the firm of a textile manufacturer. He married the director's widow, who on her death left him a comfortable fortune. Judging from the frequency of Mozart's requests for money, and from the immediacy of Puchberg's granting these requests, we can conclude that some form of agreement had been made whereby Puchberg agreed to lend Mozart money whenever he needed it. There was, perhaps, a proviso agreed upon that these requests should not exceed a certain amount at any given time. Puchberg was a keen musician, and he obviously was aware of Mozart's supreme genius. When Mozart was visiting Berlin and other German towns in 1789, it is probable that Constanze and their son Karl were living with the Puchbergs. The letters that Mozart wrote to this generous friend are certainly revealing in their open admission of Mozart's financial struggles. But they tell us nothing that explains convincingly why he should find himself in this position.

In addition to the requests themselves Mozart includes the following revealing and intriguing remarks:

June 27th 1788

Dearest, most beloved friend!

I am very much distressed that your circumstances at the moment prevent you from assisting me as much as I could wish, for my position is so serious that I am unavoidably obliged to raise money somehow. [Only ten days earlier Puchberg had sent Mozart 200 gulden.] But, good God, in whom can I confide? In no-one but you, my best friend! ... During the ten days since I came to live here, I have done more work than in two months in my former apartment, and if such black thoughts did not come to me so often, thoughts which I banish by a tremendous effort, things would be even better, for my rooms are pleasant – comfortable – and – *cheap*.

Vienna, July 12th 1789

Great God! I would not wish my worst enemy to be in my present position. And if you, most beloved friend and brother, forsake me, we are altogether lost, both my unfortunate and blameless self and my poor sick wife and child ... Owing to my unfortunate illness [rheumatic pains] I have been prevented from earning anything. But I must mention that, in spite of my wretched condition, I decided to give subscription concerts at home in order to be able to meet at least my present great and frequent expenses, for I was absolutely convinced of your friendly assistance. But even this has failed. Unfortunately Fate is so much against me, *though only in Vienna*, that even when I want to, I cannot make any money. A fortnight ago I sent round a list for subscribers and so far the only name on it is that of Baron van Swieten! Now that my dear little wife seems to be improving every day, I should be able to set to work again, if this blow, this heavy blow, had not come. At last I am beginning to feel inclined for work. I am now faced, however, with misfortunes of another kind, though, it is true, only for the moment. You know *my present circumstances*, but you also know *my prospects*. So let things remain as we arranged; that is, *thus or thus*, you understand what I mean. I can hardly bring myself to despatch this letter! And yet I must! If this illness had not befallen me, I should not have been obliged to beg so shamelessly from my only friend. Yet I hope for your forgiveness, for you know both the good *and the bad prospects of my situation*. The bad is temporary; the good will certainly persist, once the momentary evil has been alleviated.

In this letter Mozart asked Puchberg to lend him 500 gulden; five days later he received 150 gulden.

July 1789

Since the time you rendered me that great and friendly service, I have been living in such *misery*, that for very grief not only have I not been able to go out, but I could not even write.

December 29th 1789

According to the present arrangement I am to receive from the theatre management next month 200 ducats [900 gulden] for my opera [*Così fan tutte*, to be performed in January, 1790]. If you can and will lend me 400 gulden until then, you will be rescuing your friend from the greatest embarrassment ... In spite of the great expense I have to incur daily, I should try to hold out until then, were it not the New Year, when I really must pay off the chemists and doctors, whom I am no longer employing, unless I wish to lose my good name ... Contrary to our arrangement, we cannot have any music at our house tomorrow – I have too much work. But I invite you, you alone, to come along on Thursday at 10 o'clock in the morning to hear a short rehearsal of my opera. I am only inviting Haydn and yourself. I shall tell you when we meet about Salieri's plots, which, however, have completely failed already.

Puchberg replied to this letter with a loan of 300 gulden, with a further 100 gulden three weeks later. Six days later the curtain went up for the first performance of *Così fan tutte*; it had been commissioned by the Emperor, Joseph II, and it delighted the Viennese. Four performances followed immediately, and there would have been more had not the Emperor died, on February 20th 1790. As a result, the theatres were closed. In April Mozart wrote the letter to Puchberg already quoted in which he revealed the need for secrecy and his fears that details about his private life might become known.

While struggling to make both ends meet with the kind assistance of Michael Puchberg, Mozart was writing letters to Constanze which show that, despite her shortcomings, he still loved her. As Michael Levey remarks in his biography, these letters do not help one decide whether Constanze loved Mozart. In fact they indicate that Constanze's affections, perhaps never intense, were beginning to wane and look for employment elsewhere.

In April and May of 1789 Mozart travelled with Prince Karl Lichnowski, a fellow Mason and composition pupil of his, to Berlin and Potsdam. The prince, an officer in the Prussian army, was making one of his regular visits to Berlin, and he invited Mozart to travel through Germany with him and to introduce him to his sovereign, Frederick William II. On the way to Berlin, they stopped in Dresden. Here Mozart played his Piano Concerto no. 26 which he had composed the year before, at the Court of Frederick Augustus, King of Saxony, and for this he was given 450 gulden. At Potsdam, all went according to plan and the king commissioned Mozart to compose two piano sonatas (K. 570, 576) and also six string quartets, with cello parts that he himself could play. Three years earlier, in 1786, Frederick William had succeeded his uncle, Frederick the Great, and had continued his active encouragement of music at court. Frederick the Great played the flute and composed many works, including 121 flute sonatas, four flute concertos, two overtures, three cantatas and several marches. Max Joseph III of Wittelsbach, Anton of Saxony and Frederick Augustus of Saxony also composed pieces for their court musicians.

While Mozart was in Berlin a performance of *The Abduction from the Seraglio* was put on in his honour. In addition to the sum he would have been paid for this, he received 700 gulden from the King of Prussia for one of the string quartets and a quintet. Whenever he received money for his compositions, biographers, as already mentioned, searching for the tragic or negative aspects, suggest that these payments could have been more. This could be said about most payments to talented authors and composers throughout history. Composition was Mozart's favourite occupation and there was nothing else he wanted to do.

When Vincent Novello visited Constanze in Salzburg in 1829, she told him that Frederick William of Prussia had invited Mozart to live at Potsdam as Court Composer. He was offered, Novello was told, the magnificent sum of 1,600 zechins or 8,000 gulden. Another figure of 4,500 gulden has been given (Grove, *Dictionary of Music*, Vol. 5). But Mozart's answer was 'no'.

All was ready, in December 1787, we learn from Niemetschek's biography (1808), for a visit to England when the Emperor made Mozart Imperial Chamber Composer. He gladly accepted and stayed in Vienna. Invitations to London followed in December 1789 and in October 1790; both were turned down, and no steps were taken to move to Prussia. We can only conclude that his financial problems were not so acute as historians have made out. There may have been an additional reason for staying in Vienna. He was urging Puchberg to keep certain facts about his private life a secret. If a close friendship with another woman was involved, this would certainly constitute an excellent reason for remaining in the capital.

In his letters to Constanze there is no reference to money borrowed from Puchberg or their need to economise, only declarations of love and requests that she should be '*careful of your honour and of mine*'. He also asked her to 'consider *appearances*', in other words, to try at least to behave as if she still loved him. He finished one letter, from Dresden (April 16th 1789) saying 'I kiss and squeeze you 1095060437082 times – now you can practise your pronunciation.' In this letter he asked if progress was being made with a portrait, presumably of Constanze herself.* This is a luxury that would not have been considered if they had been in serious financial difficulty. In some of Mozart's letters at this time he is amusingly uninhibited in telling Constanze of his love for her.

Berlin, May 19th 1789

Dearest, most beloved wife of my heart!
 . . . This time I can't write very much to you, as I have to pay some calls and I am only sending you this to announce my arrival . . . Oh, how glad I shall be to be with you again, my darling! But the first thing I shall do is to take you by your front curls; for how on earth could you think, or even imagine, that I had forgotten you? For even supposing such a thing you will get on the very first night a thorough spanking on your dear little kissable bottom; and this you can count on.

Four days later he wrote again, telling Constanze that he would be back in Vienna in ten days' time.

Berlin, May 23rd 1789

Dearest, most beloved, most precious little wife!
 . . . On June 1st I intend to sleep in Prague, and on the 4th – the 4th – with my darling little wife. Arrange your dear sweet

* This portrait has not been found.

nest very prettily, for my little fellow deserves it indeed. He has really behaved himself very well and is only longing to possess your sweetest [word deleted]. Just picture to yourself that rascal; as I write he climbs on to the table and looks at me questioningly. But the rogue is simply [word deleted] and now the knave burns only more fiercely and can hardly be restrained ...

I kiss you millions of times and am ever your most faithful husband

W. A. Mozart

In the course of this letter he mentioned that he had lent his companion, Prince Lichnowsky, 100 gulden. He pointed out to Constanze that he was 'fortunate enough to be enjoying the King's favour'. He returned home, as planned, in early June but he still had to borrow from Michael Puchberg, writing the letters already quoted. Thanks to these loans, and money from a revival of *The Marriage of Figaro* in Vienna in August, Constanze was able to go to the health resort of Baden, an hour's coach journey from the capital.

The implications of this visit to Baden, and her extended residence here during the next two years have never been examined by historians. Poor people cannot afford such comforts. These visits are clear proof that Mozart and Constanze were not miserably poor during the last three years of his life. With the money received from his commissions, his salary and the money that he borrowed, he was able to afford at least some luxuries for Constanze, if not for himself. He was in debt when he died, but the profit made from just one concert, a fortnight later more than covered the money that he owed.

As Ludwig Nohl points out in his biography, Mozart 'was better off than the other composers of his day, and it is probable that Haydn or Leopold Mozart would have managed with his income.' Wolfgang's music brought other benefits not usually available to the ordinary man. A certain Herr Rindum, a leather boiler, was so delighted by his concerts and his operas that he gave Constanze special boiled tripe baths that she needed for her foot, without charging her a penny. He also offered to have her in his house for this treatment, free of charge, for as long as she wished.*

We can gain some insight into Mozart's state of mind at this time if we look more closely at the plot and characterisation of *Così fan tutte*. In this opera, we have a study of two men and two women finding they are falling for a second lover. After composing *Don Giovanni*, Mozart resolved to write an opera in which there were two principal soprano characters, both of equal importance.

As there are two leading men in the story who change partners, each girl is abandoned by one and taken up by the other. In this way, both girls portray or represent the old or established love; both represent the newly discovered mistress. It would be reasonable to see in Constanze a real-life inspiration and model for each girl in *Così* in their roles as women already loved by the two men. It would not be unreasonable to see if there was another woman in Mozart's life who inspired him to create the roles of the two sopranos as mistresses or new loves. Thirty years later, Constanze was to tell Vincent Novello that she did not like the plot of *Così fan tutte*.†

As we have seen, what we know about Michael Puchberg, Mozart's principal financial supporter, tells us nothing about the mystery surrounding his frequent need for help. The only other letter we have, in which Mozart asks for a loan, is the one referred to at the end of chapter 3, addressed to Franz Hofdemel. Here we are given clues. They do not lead to any solution of Mozart's money problems, but we are taken directly into his private life, to his 'present circumstances' which, he told Puchberg, must remain a secret.

This is the letter Mozart wrote to Hofdemel:

Vienna, end of March 1789

Dearest Friend!

I am taking the liberty of asking you without any hesitation for a favour. I should be very much obliged to you if you could

* Ludwig Nohl, *Mozart's Leben* (Berlin) 1906.
† Vincent and Mary Novello, *A Mozart Pilgrimage*, Novello, 1955.

and would lend me a hundred gulden until the 20th of next month. On that day I receive the quarterly instalment of my salary and shall then repay the loan with thanks. I have relied too much on a sum of a hundred ducats [450 gulden] due to me from abroad. Up to the present I have not received it, although I am expecting it daily. Meanwhile I have left myself too short of cash, so that *at the moment* I greatly need some ready money and have therefore appealed to your goodness, as I am absolutely convinced of your friendship.

Well, we shall soon be able to call one another by *a more delightful name*! For your novitiate is very nearly at an end!

Mozart

Franz Hofdemel was a chancery official at the Law Court in Vienna. He had been the private secretary of Count Seilern, and had recently joined the same lodge of the Masons that Mozart had entered. Without delay he lent Mozart the 100 gulden for a period of four months. The composer was getting ready to leave Vienna and journey to Berlin with Prince Lichnowsky, so the money was probably needed for this trip. Hofdemel was an amateur musician; he often invited friends to music recitals in his elegant flat in the Grünangergasse, in Vienna. Here he installed a valuable piano, and this, together with his three violins, indicates that he played these instruments. He and Mozart attended lectures on Freemasonry together and it is most likely that Mozart's music was played at Hofdemel's parties, and that Mozart himself took part. The chancery official dressed very smartly, possessing a wardrobe of most expensive clothes. His salary was 400 gulden a year, but this did not prevent him lending Count Gottfried von Walldorf several thousand gulden. In March 1791 Hofdemel asked the count to return the sum of 4,400 gulden. This sum was probably handed over, and a further sum of 500 gulden was received by Hofdemel on November 1st of that year. Gottfried von Walldorf lived in Brünn (now Brno), sixty-five miles north of Vienna, which was on the road to Prague.

Hofdemel's wife, Maria Magdalena, was the daughter of Gotthard Pokorny, a school teacher and *Kapellmeister* at St

Peter's church in Brünn. He was a violinist and organist and had been a pupil of a celebrated musician, Wenzel Wrobek. Gotthard Pokorny was born on November 16th 1733, in Böhmisch-Brod, in Bohemia. He became a schoolmaster and later moved to Brünn. In 1760 he was made the *Kapellmeister*. His daughter, Magdalena, was born in 1766. She became proficient at the piano, and her father often took her to concerts. We do not know the exact date of her marriage to Hofdemel.

In 1789, Magdalena, now a very beautiful young woman, twenty-three-years-old, came to Mozart for piano lessons. It was, in fact, usual for Mozart to visit the houses of his pupils on these occasions, so many of the lessons were probably given in her apartment. We know that in the summer of 1790 Mozart had only two pupils. He wrote to Puchberg telling him this, adding that he would like to have more. In this same letter he asked for another loan.

Vienna, May 17th 1790

You know how things are with me; in short, as I can find no true friends to help me, I am obliged to resort to moneylenders; but as it takes time to seek out the most Christian among this un-Christian class of people, I am at the moment so destitute that I must beg you, dearest friend, in the name of all that is sacred to assist me. If, as I hope to do, I get the money in a week or a fortnight, I shall at once repay what you lend me now. Alas, I must still ask you to wait patiently for the sums I have already been owing you for such a long time. If you only knew what grief and worry all this causes me. It has prevented me all this time from finishing my quartets.* I now have great hopes of an appointment at court, for I have reliable information that the Emperor has not sent back my petition with a favourable or damning remark, as he has the others, but has retained it. That is a good sign. Next Saturday, I intend to perform my quartets at home, and request the pleasure of your company and that of your wife.

* K. 589, 590, for Frederick William II. For these quartets he was given 1,600 gulden.

I now have two pupils and should very much like to raise the number to eight. Do your best to spread the news that I am willing to give lessons.

Without delay Puchberg let Mozart have 150 gulden. On previous occasions when Mozart mentioned his pupils, he gave their names. This time no names were given. One of the two piano pupils was a physician, Joseph Frank, but he was given only twelve lessons.* Wolfgang's second unnamed pupil was Magdalena Hofdemel.

When Mozart wrote to Franz Hofdemel, her husband, asking for a loan of 100 gulden, he was about to set out on his journey to Berlin and the Court of Frederick William II. Taking the part of Blonde in the production of *The Abduction from the Seraglio* in Berlin, when Mozart was there, was Henrietta Baranius, a beautiful girl who had been, briefly, a mistress of Frederick William himself. According to Mozart's early biographers, Jahn and Nohl, there is reason to believe that this talented soprano and the composer may have enjoyed a sexual relationship. After his death Constanze admitted that Mozart was not always faithful to her. He told her that he had occasionally indulged in sexual flirtations with maids. Constanze claimed that she forgave him. But sometimes there were bitter arguments.†

When Mozart returned to Vienna from Berlin, his main preoccupation was work on a revised version of *The Marriage of Figaro* for production in Vienna during the summer of this year, 1789. Cast in the role of Susanna, the maid employed by the Countess, the girl who marries Figaro, was Adriana Ferrarese, the mistress of Lorenzo da Ponte, Mozart's librettist. In one of his letters to Constanze, Mozart says 'I have just lunched with Madame Ferraresi at her house. The little aria

---

* Deutsches Museum, Leipzig, 1854. Vol. 2, p. 27. A seventeen-year-old boy, Josef Wölfl, from Salzburg, later called himself a 'pupil of Mozart', but this may have meant that he had violin lessons from Leopold Mozart. *Mozart Jahrbuch* (Salzburg, 1962/63), p. 126.

† Ludwig Nohl, p. 450; Schurig, *Mozart* (1922) vol. 2, p. 294.

which I composed for her* ought, I think, to be a success. She liked it very much.' Mozart and da Ponte chose Adriana for the important role of Fiordiligi in their new opera, *Così fan tutte*, which was first performed in January of the following year.

Another soprano who took part in Mozart's operas was the beautiful Caterina Cavalieri, the mistress of Antonio Salieri, the Court *Kapellmeister*. She was an Austrian, a singer of great merit, who had taken the role of Constanze in *The Abduction from the Seraglio* in 1782, in Mozart's *The Impresario*,† as Madame Silberklang, in 1786, as Donna Elvira, in *Don Giovanni* two years later, and in Mozart's arrangement of Handel's *Acis and Galatea*, also in 1788. A good friend also of Mozart's at this time was Emanuel Schikaneder, who ran a theatre in Vienna, the Wieden, and who wrote the libretto of *The Magic Flute* in 1790. He had several mistresses and an uncounted number of children by them. If Mozart now took a mistress, he would not, in such company, have been the odd man out.

In June 1790 Mozart was able to report to Puchberg that Constanze was in slightly better health. The doctor, however, was recommending a course of sixty baths at Baden, where she now was. In addition, he told his friend, she would have to take a further course at this resort later in the year. Mozart was able to afford these extended stays in Baden, with his now regular salary and occasional small loans from Puchberg. If he had been as poor as his letters to Puchberg – taken by themselves – make out, such an enjoyable and leisurely convalescence would have been out of the question.

He was able to write a cheerful letter to Constanze from Frankfurt, where he stayed for the first half of October 1790, when his new sovereign, Leopold II, was crowned there as Holy Roman Emperor. Mozart had taken with him Franz Hofer, who two years earlier had married Constanze's sister, Josefa. Like Aloysia Weber, Josefa was an excellent soprano;

---

* K. 579. '*Un moto di gioia*', a tumult of joy.
† For *The Impresario* Mozart received 225 gulden.

she took the part of the Queen of the Night at the first
performance of *The Magic Flute* in the autumn of 1791. Her
husband was a good violinist.

Frankfurt, September 28th 1790

Dearest, most beloved little wife of my heart!

We have just stopped at an inn in the suburb of Sach-
senhausen, and are in the seventh heaven of delight at having
secured a room. The journey was very enjoyable, and we had
fine weather, except on one day.... At Regensburg we lunched
magnificently to the accompaniment of divine music; we had
angelic cooking and some glorious Moselle wine. At Wurz-
burg, a fine, magnificent town, we fortified our precious
stomachs with coffee. The food was tolerable everywhere, but
at Aschaffenburg, mine host was kind enough to fleece us
disgracefully.

I am longing for news of you, of your health, our affairs and
so forth. I am fully resolved to make as much money as I can
here and then return to you with great joy. What a glorious life
we shall have then! I will work – work so hard – that no
unforseen accidents shall ever reduce us to such desperate
straits again. I should like you to get Stadler to send ... to you
about that matter. His last suggestion was that the money
should be advanced on Hoffmeister's draft alone, that is, 1,000
gulden in cash and the remainder in cloth. Then everything
could be paid off, we should have a little over, and on my return
I should have nothing to do but work. The whole business
could be settled by a friend with carte blanche from me. Adieu.
I kiss you a thousand times.

Ever your
Mzt

This tells us more about Mozart's finances than most of his
letters to Constanze, but it still leaves many questions unanswered. Franz Anton Hoffmeister was a music publisher
and composer. He published several minor works of Mozart
and helped him with a loan of 10 gulden in 1785. While in
Frankfurt, and on his way back, staying at Mainz, Mannheim,

Linz and Munich, Mozart gave Constanze further instructions about Hoffmeister's financial assistance: 'For safety's sake I should very much like to raise 2,000 gulden on Hoffmeister's draft. But you will have to give some other reason; you may say, for example, that I am making some speculation about which you know nothing' ... A week later:

> If the business with Hoffmeister is at least so far advanced that *only my presence is required*, then, after deducting interest at the rate of 20%, I shall have 1,600 out of 2,000 gulden. I can then pay out 1,000 gulden and shall have 600 left. Well, I shall begin to give little quartet subscription concerts in Advent and I shall also take some pupils. I need never repay the sum, *as I am composing* for Hoffmeister – so everything will be quite in order. But please settle the affair with Hoffmeister, that is, if you really want me to return ... Do your best with the help of *Red-currant face* [the clarinettist, Anton Stadler, for whom Mozart wrote his Clarinet Quintet (K. 581) and the Clarinet Concerto] *or someone else to conclude that business with Hoffmeister* and to make known generally my intention to take pupils. Then we shall certainly have enough to live on.

A fortnight later: 'Get things going so that that affair with Hoffmeister may be concluded.'

At Frankfurt *The Marriage of Figaro* was performed and Mozart played two of his piano concertos at a concert; at Mannheim he attended a production of *Figaro* and gave a recital before the Elector, Prince Karl Theodor, for which he received 135 gulden; at Munich he took part in a concert given by the Elector in honour of the King of Naples and Sicily. 'It is greatly to the credit of the Viennese Court that the King has to hear me in a foreign country,' he wrote to Constanze. The King of Naples might have expected to hear Mozart play in Vienna on September 19th, before he left for Frankfurt, when his two daughters, Maria Theresa and Louise, married two of the Austrian Emperor's sons, Francis and Ferdinand, but no music by Mozart was chosen. 'I am famous, admired and popular here,' Mozart wrote from Frankfurt; 'on the other hand the Frankfurt people are even more stingy than the Viennese.' At Mannheim 'the whole cast [of *The Marriage of Figaro*] implored me to stay on and help them with the rehearsals.' And in Munich he was delighted to find himself so popular; 'you cannot conceive what a fuss they are making of me.'

In the letters that Mozart wrote to Constanze during this German tour, there is a new element of dissatisfaction which jars with his declarations of love for her and with his confident forecasts of continued happiness together.

Frankfurt, September 30th 1790

Dearest little wife of my heart!

... I am as excited as a child at the thought of seeing you again. If people could see into my heart, I should almost feel ashamed. To me everything is cold – cold as ice. Perhaps if you were with me I might possibly take more pleasure in the kindness of those I meet here. But, as it is, everything seems so empty. Adieu, my love, I am ever your husband, who loves you with all his soul,

Mozart

Frankfurt, October 3rd 1790

Dearest, most beloved little wife!

At last I feel comforted and happy. First of all, because I have had news from you, my love, news for which I was simply aching; and secondly, on account of the reassuring information about my affairs. I have now made up my mind to compose at once the Adagio for the watchmaker [Count Josef Deym, for his mechanical organ (K. 594)], and then to slip a few ducats into the hand of my dear little wife ... Every morning I stay indoors in my hole of a bedroom and compose. My sole recreation is the theatre, where I meet several friends from Vienna, Munich, Mannheim and even Salzburg. This is the way I should like best of all to go on living – but – I fear that it will soon come to an end and that I am in for a restless life. Already I am being invited everywhere – and however tiresome it may be to let myself be on view, I see nevertheless how necessary it is. So in God's name I submit to it...

Frankfurt, October 8th 1790

If you could only look into my heart. There a struggle is going on between my yearning and longing to see and embrace you once more and my desire to bring home a large sum of money. I have often thought of travelling *farther afield*, but whenever I tried to bring myself to take the decision, the thought always came to me, how bitterly I should regret it, if I were to separate myself from my beloved wife for *such an uncertain prospect, perhaps to no purpose whatever*. I feel I had left you years ago. If you were with me I might perhaps decide more easily, but I am too much accustomed to you and I love you too dearly to endure being separated from you for long. Besides, all this talk about the Imperial towns is mere misleading chatter.

Frankfurt, October 15th 1790

I seem to notice that you doubt my eagerness to write to you, and this pains me bitterly. Surely you ought to know me better. Good God! Only love me half as much as I love you, and I shall be content.

While I was writing the last page, tear after tear fell on the paper. But I must cheer up – catch! An astonishing number of kisses are flying about – I see a whole crowd of them! Ha! Ha! I have just caught three – They are delicious!

While Mozart was away in Germany, Constanze was able to pursue the important financial transaction as requested in his letters to her. When he returned he signed a promissory note, acknowledging receipt of 1,000 gulden, a loan from Heinrich Lackenbacher, a Viennese merchant, for a two year period, with five per cent interest.* Neither Lackenbacher nor Hoff-

---

* Otto Deutsch, *Mozart, a Documentary Biography* (Black, 1965), pp. 371–2.

meister claimed repayment after Mozart's death. This loan was the equivalent of a year and a quarter's salary, so this must have made life for him and Constanze a lot easier.

On November 16th of the previous year, 1789, Constanze had given birth to her fifth child, Anna. After only one hour of life, she died of cramp. Now, when Mozart returned from Frankfurt, about November 10th, Constanze was perhaps pregnant again. He had been away for seven weeks. Constanze's baby was born on July 26th 1791; conception, therefore, probably occurred towards the end of October 1790. In the last week of that month, Mozart left Mannheim and travelled to Munich. He had been away from Vienna for nearly five weeks,* he would not be returning home for another fortnight. Staying with Constanze at the time was Franz Xaver Süssmayr a twenty-four-year-old student of composition. When the baby was born, he was named Franz Xaver Wolfgang Mozart. Constanze's other children were given the Christian names of their godfather; Franz Xaver's godfather was Johann Thomas von Trattner. The second and third children of Constanze were named Karl Thomas and Johann Thomas; Trattner was also their godfather. For this reason perhaps his names had not been given to the new baby. Thirty-nine years later, the English music publisher Vincent Novello and his wife, Mary, met Constanze and Franz Xaver, her son, in Salzburg, and reported that he looked like Mozart, but we do not know that Süssmayr was strikingly dissimilar to Mozart in appearance: we have no portrait or description of him. In his biography of Mozart, Nissen, Constanze's second husband, makes a point of the son's likeness to Mozart: 'The features and ears of the son, Wolfgang [his third name], are like those of his father. What was extraordinarily noticeable was the shape of Mozart's ears, quite different from the usual, a shape which only his younger son inherited.'

It cannot be said that Franz Xaver Wolfgang inherited any

* Mozart left Vienna on September 22nd 1970. See letter from Frankfurt, dated September 28th 1790. 'The journey has only taken us six days.'

real musical talent as a composer or player. The son of a genius is not automatically talented but the child's limited talent may be significant.

After Mozart's death Constanze refused to give Süssmayr the score of the Requiem for completion, thereby ignoring her husband's instructions. It was given instead to Josef Eybler. All she said about this was that she felt angry (*böse*) with Süssmayr for reasons unstated. According to Dietrich Schickling, writing in the *Mozart Jahrbuch*, in 1976, there is reason to believe that she wished to marry him.

Mozart obviously had something to complain about. His admonitions were deeply felt. When he was in Dresden, in April 1789, he begged Constanze, in the letter already quoted, to be careful of her honour and to consider *appearances*. In August, four months later, he told her that 'she was too free and easy with ...' (in the letter also quoted).

> A woman must always make herself respected, or else people will begin to talk about her. My love! Forgive me for being so frank, but my peace of mind demands it as well as our mutual happiness. Remember that you yourself once admitted to me that you were inclined to *comply too easily*. You know the consequences of that. Remember too the promise you gave to me. Oh, God, do try, my love! Rest assured that it is only by her prudent behaviour that a wife can enchain her husband.

In a letter from Berlin written on May 23rd 1789, he listed and dated all the letters he had sent her since leaving Vienna, and listed and dated the six letters he had received from her. Not a single letter that Constanze wrote to Mozart has been preserved.

A year later, in October 1790, from Frankfurt, he was imploring her to 'love me half as much as I love you'. If she could do that, he would be content.

There is, of course, no reason why, when Constanze's sixth child was born, in July 1791, Mozart should have thought that he was not the father. He may well have been, if the baby was a fortnight early. There is no evidence that he objected to the baby being christened Franz Xaver, so he probably felt that he could be the father. But if conception had occurred the full nine months earlier, the father must have been Süssmayr. Indeed, Constanze herself might not have known for certain who the father was.

References to Süssmayr in Mozart's letters were often made illegible by a later hand, presumably Constanze's. Many years later, on May 31st 1837, she gave the Abbé Maximilian Stadler a brief explanation of her extraordinary decision to give the manuscript of the Requiem to Josef Eybler instead of Süssmayr:

> I gave Eybler the task of finishing the Requiem because at that time I was angry [*böse*] with him [Süssmayr]; I don't know why. Mozart himself thought a lot of Eybler, and I thought that a person such as he could do it. So I asked Eybler to come and see me, and told him of my wishes. But, since he refused straight away, he didn't get it in his hand.

This last remark is not true. Eybler *was* given the manuscript. In this letter to Stadler, Constanze suggests that her anger against Süssmayr was temporary, but immediately after the death of Mozart, Süssmayr left her and never saw her again. He died in 1803.

Constanze's frequent absence from her husband in the last three years of his life, the total absence of any letter from her to him, and her conduct at Baden, which clearly irritated Mozart, all indicate that she did not love him sincerely during these last few years. When he died, she would have felt completely free to marry another man. In the last two years of Mozart's life, she had shared her apartment in Vienna and at Baden contentedly, it seems, with Süssmayr. It is therefore reasonable to assume that she may well have hoped to continue to live with him as his wife. But immediately Mozart died, Constanze would have appeared to Süssmayr in a new light. She was no longer the wife of his master and employer. Overnight she had become the widow of a great man, who now was looking for a second husband. Marriage to her was not what he wanted. He left at once and never returned.

Eybler wrote the instrumental parts of the sequence leading up to the *Confutatis* and added two of his own bars to the final eight of the *Lacrimosa* in the soprano chorus. Feeling uneasy about Constanze's decision to ignore Süssmayr, he did not trust himself with any further composition. He did not give the manuscript back to Constanze but to Abbé Stadler. In the end, Süssmayr completed the work, but exact knowledge of who wrote what is not possible.

By far the most important work created by Mozart in 1790, the year before he died, was his Piano Concerto, no. 27 (K. 595). His output during this year was unusually small – an overture and three country dances for orchestra, a Minuet in D for piano, a string quintet (K. 593), for Count Walsegg, and an adagio and allegro for mechanical organ, a composition which he found tedious, because of the limited range of this instrument. He completed his two string quartets for King Frederick William II of Prussia – and wrote the piano concerto, which he finished on January 5th the following year. He was now making smaller requests for loans for Puchberg;* in October or November he was given the loan of 1,000 gulden by Lackenbacher; he felt financially strong enough to turn down two invitations to London;† to bring in more money he gave piano lessons, which he professed not to enjoy. But at this time there were only two pupils, and one of them was the beautiful Magdalena Hofdemel. With Constanze at Baden for weeks at a time from August 1789 to the autumn of 1791, Mozart had

---

* In 1790 Puchberg's loans to Mozart were: 25, 25, 150, 25, 25, 100, 150, 25 and 10 gulden. In 1791 there were two loans of 30 and 25 gulden.

† By Robert O'Reilly, manager of an Italian opera company, and Johann Saloman, the German impresario, who brought Haydn to London in 1791.

In the spring of 1791, we learn from the *Memoirs* of Lorenzo da Ponte: 'I had a talk with Mozart and strove to persuade him to go with me to London. But a short time previously he had received a life pension from the Emperor Joseph in recognition of his divine operas; and he was then setting to music a German opera, *The Magic Flute*, from which he was hoping for new glories. He asked for six months' time to make up his mind.'

ample cause for feeling lonely, but she was only seventeen miles away. If he had wanted to, he could have stayed with her and Süssmayr at Baden. Their son, Karl, was conveniently out of the way at a boarding school. But Mozart preferred to stay in Vienna, making only brief visits to Baden. He preferred to compose at home, near his friend, Emanuel Schikaneder, manager of the Theater auf der Widen, who commissioned him to write *The Magic Flute*, and near Magdalena, whose comfortable flat was only five minutes' walk away.

Soon after Mozart's death, in 1804, Jean-Baptiste-Antoine Suard published his *Anecdotes sur Mozart* in Paris. 'Mozart,' he wrote, 'loved his wife tenderly, although he was sometimes unfaithful to her. His fancies had such a hold over him that he could not resist them.'

What can we learn about Mozart's life at this time from the beautiful piano concerto he was composing? C. M. Girdlestone, in his profound study, *Mozart's Piano Concertos*, describes this work in these words:

> The intimate nature of its feeling makes almost chamber music of it. Its proper environment is a circle of lovers of music – and of Mozart, gathered in the house of one of them. We do not know for what occasion it was written. It is generally agreed that Mozart composed it for his own use, but there is no proof of this, and the existence of cadenzas and its introspective character would lead us to think that it had been produced for a pupil.
>
> If Mozart had had to play it himself, it seems to us that he would have written a more brilliant work, like the concertos composed for his own use in 1784, 1785 and 1786. It will be remembered that the most intimate concertos of 1784 were those he wrote for others [Babette Ployer and Maria Theresa Paradis].

The comments about this concerto by Arthur Hutchings, in his *Companion to Mozart's Piano Concertos*, point in the same direction: 'No correspondence reveals the occasion for which this concerto was written. The small orchestra, a certain reserve about all its music suggest an intimate circle, rather than the formal public concert. The Larghetto (second movement) has unusual intimacy.'

This concerto is one of the most romantic creations in the whole history of art. It is great night music, inspired by love from the first quiet, seductive notes to the last, when the orchestra and the soloist combine in happiness and unison.*

Mozart's creative energy in 1791, the last year of his life, was magnificent. He wrote two operas, *The Magic Flute* and *La Clemenza di Tito*, the superb Clarinet Concerto, for his friend, Anton Stadler, the serenely consoling motet, *Ave Verum Corpus* (K. 618) for Anton Stoll, the choir master at Baden, another string quartet (K. 614) for Count Walsegg, an Adagio and Rondo (K. 617) for glass harmonica, flute, oboe, viola and cello, for another blind pianist, Marianne Kirchgessner, many *Kontretanze* (country dances) for orchestra, and his uncompleted Requiem, also for Count Walsegg. None of these works shows any decline in vitality, drive or originality.

Throughout this year he continued to write to Constanze with his usual expressions of affection. But on more than one occasion he suggested to her that she might as well remain at Baden if she wanted to. We might have expected him to express some dejection if he had found that Constanze now loved Süssmayr; this would be the natural reaction from a husband in his position. But if Mozart was himself in love with another woman he would not have found Constanze's conduct insupportable. In fact he would have found it advantageous if she remained at the health resort. The following remarks in Mozart's letters certainly indicate that, although he still loved her, he would be quite happy if she remained away.

Vienna, July 2nd 1791

Ma très chère Epouse!
    I trust that you are very well. I have just remembered that

---

* This concerto received its first public performance on March 4th with Mozart as soloist in the concert hall owned by the Court Caterer, Jahn, near the centre of Vienna.

you have *very seldom* been upset during pregnancy ... *Seriously* – I had much rather you would prolong your cure well into the autumn. Please tell that idiotic fellow Süssmayer to send me my score of the first act [of *The Magic Flute*] so that I may orchestrate it ... Take care of your health, for as long as you are well and are kind to me, I don't care a fig if everything else goes wrong.

Ever your Mozart

Vienna, July 5th 1791

Dearest, most beloved little Wife!

Do not be melancholy, I beg you! I hope you received the money. It is surely better for your foot that you should stay on at Baden, for there you can go out more easily. I hope to hold you in my arms on Saturday, perhaps sooner. As soon as my business here is over, I shall be with you, for I mean to take a long rest in your arms; and indeed I shall need it, for this mental worry and anxiety and all the running about connected with it is really exhausting me. ... [name deleted] is with me at the moment. He has a penchant for you and is perfectly certain that you must have noticed it.

We do not know what Mozart was referring to when he mentions 'all the running about'. Two days later he again refers to this matter, and again expresses a feeling of dissatisfaction.

Vienna, July 7th 1791

Dearest, most beloved little Wife!

You will forgive me, I know, for only sending you *one letter* a day. The reason is that I must keep hold of ... and not let him escape. I am at his house every day at seven o'clock in the morning. I did not go to see the balloon,* for it is the sort of thing which one can imagine. Besides, I thought that this time too nothing would come of it ...

* François Blanchard (1753–1809) ascended in his Montgolfier balloon on July 6th 1791 from the Prater and landed in Gross-Enzersdorf, just outside the capital. He had made two unsuccessful attempts in Vienna on March 9th and May 29th.

My one wish now is that my affairs should be settled, so that
I can be with you again. You cannot imagine how I have been
aching for you all this long while. I can't describe what I have
been feeling – a kind of emptiness, which hurts me dreadfully –
a kind of longing, which is never satisfied, which never ceases,
and which persists, or rather increases daily. When I think how
merry we were together at Baden – like children – and what
sad, weary hours I am spending here! Even my work gives me
no pleasure, because I am accustomed to stop working now
and then and exchange a few words with you. Alas! this
pleasure is no longer possible. If I go to the piano and sing
something out of my opera, I have to stop at once, for this stirs
my emotions too deeply. Basta! The very hour after I finish this
business, I shall be off and away from here. I have no news to
tell you.

                                              Ever your
                                              Mozart

Only two days later he asked her again if she would like to
remain at Baden.

                                    Vienna, July 9th 1791

Dearest, most beloved little Wife!

   Your letter of yesterday made me feel so depressed that I
almost made up my mind to let that business slide and drive out
to you. But what good would it have done? I should only have
had to drive back again at once or, instead of being happy, I
should have been most dreadfully worried. The affair must be
concluded in a few days, for . . .'s promises were really serious
and solemn. Then I shall go straight to you. But if you prefer it,
I shall send you the money you need, and you can then pay
everything and return to Vienna. There is nothing I should like
better.

   At the same time I do think that in this fine weather Baden
must be very pleasant for you and most beneficial to your
health, as there are such glorious walks there. You yourself
must feel this more than anyone. So if you find that the air and
exercise thoroughly agree with you, do stay on. I shall come
and fetch you or, if you like, spend a few days with you. But, as

I have already said, if you would rather do so, return to Vienna
tomorrow. Tell me quite frankly which you prefer. I kiss you
millions of times and am ever your

Mozart

It was about this time, in early August 1791, that Magdalena
Hofdemel conceived her second son; he was born on May 10th
1792. Constanze's baby, Franz Xaver Wolfgang, was born on
July 26th 1791. We might therefore have expected some reference to this latter event in Mozart's letters. But no letters to or
from Mozart, written between July 12th and October 7th
1791, have survived. In the published editions of his letters
there is no explanation, or comment of any kind, to account
for this sudden three-months' silence – only a reference to
Mozart's visit, with Constanze and Süssmayr to Prague at the
end of August for the first performance of *La Clemenza di Tito*.
It had been commissioned by the Bohemian nobility as a grand
occasion during the coronation festivities of the new Emperor,
Leopold II, as King of Bohemia.

Constanze gave her son the first two names of the man who
may have been his father, Franz Xaver Süssmayr. Magdalena
Hofdemel named her son Johann Alexander Franz. Her husband, by that time, was dead, having committed suicide. It was
therefore her decision to give her child that first name. The
first two names are those of the man who stood as godfather
at the christening, the Royal Appellation Chancellor, Fidel
Holderer. The first name, Johann, was also the first Christian
name of Mozart.

5

The Death of Mozart
1791

TAMINO This portrait has a magical beauty; this divine image fills my heart with a new joy! I would draw her gently to me, and eternally she would be mine! I will embrace her, even though it may mean my death.

THE MAGIC FLUTE *1791*

IN JUNE 1791, during a walk in the Prater in Vienna with Constanze, Mozart declared that he had been poisoned. 'Someone has given me aqua toffana,' he said.* This was a poison, well known in the eighteenth century as an effective way of killing with impunity, as the poison worked slowly, leaving symptoms that could be diagnosed as signs of natural ailments. It was invented in the previous century by a Sicilian woman, Teofania di Adamo and her daughter, Julia, of Naples. In 1659 the Roman police mounted an investigation into the deaths of a number of men, who, it was discovered, were poisoned by their wives. They had all been dispatched by doses of aqua toffana. The two inventors were arrested in Rome in the same year.

This poison is a mixture of white arsenic, antimony and lead oxide. The effect is gradual, resulting in death only after several months. Some poisons cause a general swelling of the body; this can be an effect of aqua toffana. Like mercury, which causes uraemia, it can escape detection by a doctor.

It was at this time that Mozart was commissioned to write a Requiem by Count Franz Walsegg-Stuppach. He was already at work on *The Magic Flute* for Emanuel Schikaneder and another opera, *La Clemenza di Tito* for the Bohemian nobility, two commissions which brought in money and morale-boosting prestige. There was no need for anxiety or depression, but this third commission, for Walsegg, may have perplexed him. On February 14th 1791 the count's wife died

* Vincent and Mary Novello, *A Mozart Pilgrimage*, pp. 125-28, 345. Franz Niemeczek, *Mozart* (Prague 1978).

and the music-loving but eccentric widower resolved to mark the anniversary of her death with a fitting composition. Wishing to appear as both patron and composer, the count indulged in a real-life melodrama of his own construction. He sent his estate-manager, Ignaz Leutgeb, to Mozart with instructions that his own name should not be divulged. The commission was at once accepted and the first payment of 225 gulden received. Another 225 gulden would be paid when the work was completed. There is no reference in Mozart's letters which indicate any reluctance to compose this work, or that it worried him in any way. In spite of the incentive, Mozart had written only half, or less than half, by the time of his death, some six months later. As he had already written fifteen masses, Count Walsegg could have reckoned that one more would not present any difficulty and that it would be completed in a month or two. One can only conclude that Mozart found other work more attractive. Only three weeks before his death he wrote a triumphant masonic cantata, *Laut verkunde unser Freude* (*Loudly proclaim our Joy*), and he never abandoned his calm, detached, philosophical acceptance of death as a friend, not an enemy, of life. As Michael Levey says, in his biography of Mozart, this Requiem 'is more likely to have prompted thoughts of life' than gloomy indulgence in self-pity. The notion that Mozart looked on the Requiem introspectively as a foreshadow of his own death is, in the opinion of another biographer, Ivor Keys, 'historically suspect'.

Mozart's compositions during this last year show that he was in fact advancing into new and wider realms of the imagination, into the realms of Isis and Osiris, in *The Magic Flute*, into the Masonic world of brotherhood, as a divine, but not necessarily Christian, fellowship, into the similar concepts of Zarathustra, who appears, it seems, as Sarastro in *The Magic Flute*, and into the nineteenth and twentieth century world of machinery and new instruments, with his Fantasy for Mechanical Organ (K. 608) and the Adagio and Rondo for glass harmonica.

Mozart first heard this instrument when he was in London

in 1764, when it was played by Marianne Davies. In one of Leopold Mozart's letters, dated 1773, we learn that Wolfgang had played it, and that Leopold would like to possess one. It was invented in 1762 by Benjamin Franklin. Musical glasses were popular at the time; they were played by a light touch on the rims. Franklin mounted the glasses horizontally in scale, so that chords and melodies could be played more easily. This invention was popular until the 1820s; with its purity of tone it was the forerunner of the celeste and today's electronic instruments.

At the end of August 1791, Mozart, Constanze and Süssmayr journeyed to Prague for the first performance, on September 6th of *La Clemenza di Tito*, for the coronation festivities arranged in honour of Leopold II. For this Mozart was paid 900 gulden. One member of the audience, Count Zinzendorf, found it 'most tedious'; another, the Empress, Maria Luisa of Naples, found it too serious, dismissing it as 'a piece of German rubbish'. But Anton Stadler, the clarinettist, reported that audiences greeted it with 'tremendous applause.'

At the first performance were Franz von Kleist and his nephew Heinrich, who later found fame as a novelist and a poet. Mozart's melodies, wrote Kleist, 'are so beautiful as to entice the angels down to earth.' After a performance of *Don Giovanni* in Prague four days earlier, he declared Mozart 'will move future generations when the bones of kings have long since mouldered away.' The enthusiastic applause from the audience 'must be a fine and heavenly reward for the artist who can take from the spheres their harmony and delight men's souls with his tones.'*

In 1956, on January 12th, it was reported in the Austrian papers that a watch once owned by Mozart had been discovered. The composer had borrowed some money from an ancestor of the Czech collector, who had just died, and who owned this watch. The ancestor was Magdalena's father, Gotthard Pokorny, and it had been given to him by Mozart as a security for the loan in 1791. Mozart would have been in

* Franz von Kleist, *Phantasien auf einer Reine nach Prag* (Dresden) 1792.

Brünn on his way to Prague in late August and on the way back to Vienna in the middle of September. This gold watch, made in Vienna, is wound by a small key, and it still gives the correct time (*Die Weltpresse*, Vienna, March 24th 1956). Constanze and her second husband, Georg Nissen, Mozart's biographer, never mentioned this loan, just as neither made a single mention of any member of the Pokorny or the Hofdemel family.

Constanze and Nissen never referred to another episode in Mozart's life which sheds some light on one of the questions raised by an examination of the composer's career – why did he not receive a really lucrative official appointment? Another question may be asked in this connection. What can we deduce from the reaction shown by Viennese officials when Mozart did apply for an official position?

On April 26th 1791, Mozart applied for the post of assistant *Kapellmeister* at St Stephen's cathedral, in Vienna. The *Kapellmeister* was Leopold Hofmann, who was now sixty-one. On his retirement or death, his assistant would take his place – and his salary of 2,000 gulden a year.

Mozart's deferential application for this unpaid position was immediately rejected – and then granted. What was the reason for this unfriendly reaction and for the subsequent decision to reverse it? There could have been no question of his ability to fill the post. It could only be that the authorities knew something about his private life which discouraged them from giving him this church appointment. Someone later must have persuaded them to change their minds.

Here is Mozart's application in full:

Vienna, April 26th 1791

Most honourable, Most learned
Municipal Councillors of Vienna,
Most worthy Gentlemen!
  When *Kapellmeister* Hofmann was ill, I thought of venturing to apply for his post; for my musical talents, my works and my skill in composition are well known in foreign countries, and

my name is treated everywhere with some respect, indeed – I was myself appointed several years ago composer of the distinguished Court. I hoped therefore that I was not unworthy of this post, and that I deserved the favour of the enlightened municipal council.

However *Kapellmeister* Hofmann has regained his health, and in the circumstances, for I wish him from my heart a long life, it has occurred to me that it might perhaps be of service to the Cathedral, and, most worthy gentlemen, to your advantage, if for the time being I were to be attached as unpaid assistant to the ageing *Kapellmeister* and were to have the opportunity of helping this worthy man in his office, thus gaining the approval of our learned municipal council by the actual performance of services which I may justly consider myself capable of rendering on account of my thorough knowledge of the ecclesiastical style of music.

Your most humble servant,

> Wolfgang Amade Mozart
> Royal and Imperial Court
> Composer

This document is not written in Mozart's hand, and the signature is not Mozart's. It is no doubt a master-copy which he used for drawing up his own application. The master-copy has survived, but not the letter signed by the composer. This application is clearly dated April 26th 1791. Mozart might have handed it in to the Magistrate's office on the same day, or the day after. Only a day later, on April 28th, the Magistrate's secretary, Franz Hübner, rejected this application, in the following words:

> Again it is decided [*Wieder hinauszugeben*], especially since the *Kapellmeister* at St. Stephen's Church has not at present requested an assistant, that this request cannot be granted.
>
> > from the Magistrate's Council,
> > Vienna   28th April 1791
> > Hübner, Secr.

Mozart's request for this unpaid post was thus rejected

instantly, clearly for some definite reason. The secretary must have had instructions that such an attempt to secure this church appointment must be blocked immediately. No objections were made when the post was given to Hofmann and his successor, Albrechtsberger, but the internationally famous Mozart was considered unsuitable. It is not known why Hübner said that this refusal had *again* been decided upon; Mozart had not, as far as we know, applied for this post before.

This was not the end of the mystery. The five lines of Hübner's refusal were inked over and, twelve days later, on May 9th, Mozart was given the post of assistant *Kapellmeister* on condition that he agreed to be content with the salary of his predecessor, in the event of his death or illness. He also had to agree to whatever terms the Magistrate 'will find it necessary to determine [*zu verordnen und zu bestimmen für gut wird*]'. When, on December 12th 1791, six days after Mozart's burial, Johann Georg Albrechtsberger was made assistant *Kapellmeister*, these stipulations were not made. They were, in fact, special clauses designed for Mozart only.

It is indeed strange that there was no mention of Mozart's appointment in the Viennese papers. But it was mentioned in the *Pressburger Zeitung*. As Pressburg is thirty-five miles from Vienna, it is possible that the citizens of the capital knew nothing about the appointment. On May 21st this paper included this item of news: 'The Court Composer Mozart has been given by the Magistrate of Vienna the reversion of the post of *Kapellmeister* of St. Stephen's Church, which brings in 2,000 gulden [as salary].'

Three years later, in 1794, the *Theatre Almanach* of Vienna informed its readers that 'the immortal Mozart was made Hofmann's successor and substitute'.

If Mozart's application was initially turned down by the Magistrate because it was considered that some aspect of his private life made him an unsuitable candidate for this church appointment, someone must have supplied the authorities with compromising details. From June 1788 to November 1790 Mozart lived at 26 Währinger Strasse. Behind the house there was a beautiful garden with maple and chestnut trees, lilac and jasmine bushes. In another apartment overlooking this garden lived Josef Franz Martinoli, who was the town magistrate's councillor. He served on the same committee as the Burgermaster, Josef Georg Hörl, who signed Mozart's letter of appointment. It could be Martinoli who told Hörl of Mozart's association with Magdalena. On the other hand it could be that he was a friend of Mozart, and persuaded Hörl to give him this post after all.

If Leopold Hofmann had not recovered from his recent illness, or had died during the summer, Mozart would have then received a salary which would take care of all his debts and leave plenty over for Constanze and himself. Hofmann outlived Mozart and died two years later, in 1793. The *Kirchenmeister* of St Stephen's, Andreas Fortmoser, who held this post from 1775 to 1799, has left us no record of Mozart's appointment. He died the following year, having committed suicide. When Hofmann died, Albrechtsberger took his place without any opposition from the Magistrate.

The Magic Flute was first performed on September 30th 1791. The state of Mozart's mind at this time is clearly illustrated by his amazing coolness and freedom from anxiety when he played a joke on Schikaneder while he was on stage, taking the role of Papageno in one of the first performances. Mozart himself described this extraordinary incident in a letter he wrote to Constanze. After their successful journey to Prague, she had resumed her residence at Baden.

Vienna, October 7th 1791

... Only the desire to see you in good health made me urge you to go to Baden. I already feel lonely without you. I knew I would. If I had nothing to do, I should have gone off at once to spend the week with you; but I have *no facilities for working at Baden*, and I am anxious, as far as possible, to avoid all risk of *money difficulties*. For the most pleasant thing of all is to have a mind at peace. To achieve this, however, one must work hard; and I like hard work.

This morning I worked so hard at my composition that I went on till half past one. So I dashed off to Hofer, simply in order not to lunch alone, where I found Mamma [Constanze's mother] there too. After lunch I went home at once and composed again until it was time to go to the opera. [Joseph] Leutgeb [a horn-player, who owned a cheese shop in Vienna] begged me to take him a second time and I did so. I am taking *Mamma* tomorrow. Hofer has already given her the libretto to read. In her case what will probably happen will be that she will *see* the opera, but not *hear* it.

[name deleted] had a box this evening and applauded everything most heartily ... During Papageno's aria with the glockenspiel I went behind the scenes, as I felt a sort of impulse today to play it myself. Well, just for fun, at the point where Schikaneder has a pause, I played an arpeggio. He was startled, looked behind the wings and saw me. When he had his next pause, I played no arpeggio. This time he stopped and refused to go on. I guessed what he was thinking and again played a chord. He then struck the glockenspiel and said '*Shut up*'. Whereupon everybody laughed. I am inclined to think that this joke taught many of the audience for the first time that Papageno does not play the instrument himself.

In his letters of October 7th and 8th, Mozart described in some detail his daily life, mentioning the time spent in composition, visits to the theatre, drinking black coffee and eating 'a delicious slice of sturgeon which Don Primus, my faithful valet, has brought me'. This was Joseph Deiner, a waiter at the 'Silver Snake', an eating-house where Mozart usually went for lunch. But in these letters not the whole day is described. Sometimes he slept at the house of his brother-in-law, Franz Hofer, the violinist. Constanze wrote to Wolfgang in June, asking him if he had spent the night at another house, for he replies, on June 25th, saying 'Where did I sleep? At home, of course.'

During these summer and autumn months, Mozart's life was enriched by Emanuel Schikaneder, who put at his disposal a little summer-house, or cottage, near the theatre in which *The Magic Flute* was to be presented later in the year. This theatre lay in the grounds of Prince Stahremberg's house on the outskirts of Vienna, and here the greater part of Mozart's opera was written. This summer-house is now in the garden of the Mozarteum in Salzburg.

Schikaneder also owned a summer-house in the little village of Josefsdorf, five miles from Vienna. This refuge was also put at Mozart's disposal. Some of *The Magic Flute* was composed here. Actors and actresses from the theatre visited Mozart while he was at work on the opera and wine and champagne were drunk. This information was not given in Mozart's letters, but was subsequently revealed by Schikaneder. In the biography of Mozart written by Constanze's second husband, Georg Nissen, we read, with astonishment, that Mozart 'was the husband; he produced four children, loved truly, and, even if there were several flirtations [*gab es manche Galanterie*], his good wife gladly overlooked this.' There were, in fact, six children. 'Mozart drank champagne and tokay and lived loosely (*lebt locker*).' Nissen was, it seems, referring to this period of his life. This could be a veiled reference to his friendship with Magdalena Hofdemel. He would not take the trouble to give piano lessons, Constanze told Vincent Novello in 1829, 'to any ladies but those he was in love with'.*

A postscript added to Mozart's letter to Constanze, written on October 8th 1791, indicates that she was not particularly concerned with the day-to-day details of his existence in Vienna. Whatever the implication, it is rather a strange note, one which no writer of a fictional account of Mozart would have written: 'NB You probably sent the two pairs of yellow winter trousers along with the boots to the laundry, for Joseph and I have hunted for them in vain! Adieu.'

Mozart was delighted at the way *The Magic Flute* was received in Vienna (he was paid 450 gulden). His friends too were most enthusiastic. He was now on good terms with Salieri, who frequently expressed his admiration for the opera, while he and his mistress, Caterina Cavalieri, were sitting in Mozart's box at one of the first performances. There is no real

* *A Mozart Pilgrimage*, p. 114.

evidence that Salieri poisoned Mozart, a rumour that gained
some credence in Vienna when he himself, as an old man in a
mental home, claimed he was responsible, a claim he later
denied. Mozart was also friendly with Joseph Leutgeb, who
was helping him to arrange for a new boarding school for his
seven-year-old son, Karl. Fees for this type of school could not
have been paid if Mozart was poor. Also he would not have
been able to afford the regular payments to Leonore, Constanze's maid. The future certainly looked bright.

The way in which Mozart wrote to Constanze about Karl's
progress at school, and about his own activities, clearly indicates peace of mind and a general state of optimism.

Vienna, October 14th 1791

... At six o'clock I called in the carriage for Salieri and
Madame Cavalieri – and drove them to my box. You can
hardly imagine how charming they were and how much they
liked not only my music, but the libretto and everything. They
both said that it was an *operone* [a grand opera], worthy to be
performed for the grandest festival and before the greatest
monarch, and that they would often go to see it, as they had
never seen a more beautiful or delightful show. Salieri listened
and watched most attentively and from the overture to the last
chorus there was not a single number that did not call forth
from him a bravo! or bello! It seemed as if they could not thank
me enough for my kindness. When it was over I drove them
home and then had supper at Hofer's with Karl. Then I drove
him home and we both slept soundly. Karl was absolutely
delighted at being taken to the opera.

He is looking splendid. As far as health is concerned, he
could not be in a better place [at a boarding school at Percht-
holdsdorf], but everything else there is wretched, alas! All
they can do is to turn out a good peasant into the world. But
enough of this. As his serious studies (God help them!) do not
begin until Monday, I have arranged to keep him until after
lunch on Sunday. I told them that you would like to see him. So
tomorrow, Saturday, I shall drive out with Karl to see you.
You can then keep him, or I shall take him back to Heeger [the
headmaster] after lunch. Think it over. A month [away] can

hardly do him much harm. In the meantime the arrangement with the Piarists [a school in the suburbs of Vienna, run by a Catholic teaching order] may come to something. On the whole Karl is no worse; but at the same time he is not one whit better than he was. He still has his old bad manners; he never stops chattering just as he used to do in the past; and he is, if anything, *less inclined to learn than before*. At Perchtholdsdorf all he does is to run about in the garden for five hours in the morning and five hours in the afternoon, as he himself confessed. In short, the children do nothing but eat, drink, sleep and run wild. Leutgeb and Hofer are with me at the moment. The former is staying to supper with me ... Farewell. Ever your

　　　　　　　　　　　　　　　　　　　　Mozart

I kiss Sophie [Constanze's sister] a thousand times. Do what you like with ... [name deleted] Adieu.

This is the last letter of Mozart that has been preserved. It is most unlikely that it was the last letter that he wrote. Constanze returned to Vienna in late autumn. All continued to go well at the theatre; in November Count Zinzendorf went to the twenty-fourth performance of *The Magic Flute*, and noted that there was 'a huge audience'. With his enchanting Clarinet Concerto, written for his friend, Anton Stadler, and completed at the end of September, Mozart demonstrated that his creativity was unflagging.

In the middle of November he conducted his Masonic cantata, *Laut verkunde unser Freude*, to celebrate the opening of new premises of his lodge, which was named 'New-Crowned Hope'. This joyful paean of praise for life, for love and true companionship, could not have come from anyone who was down-hearted, disillusioned or in any way depressed. It is irrefutably an affirmation of good-will and confidence. This hopeful mood must have been greatly strengthened when he received news that some Hungarian nobles had agreed to send him an annual payment. And at the same time some of his admirers in Amsterdam raised money for a subscription to be sent to him.

It was at this moment that death, of which Mozart himself

had had a premonition in June, put an end to his hopes and dreams. After the Masonic concert he felt unwell and took to his bed. A fortnight later, on December 5th, he died. It is doubly significant that we have not a single word about his death by his wife, Constanze, who was with him every day, and not a single word – no report – by the two distinguished doctors who looked after him, Dr Thomas Closset and Dr Matthias von Sallaba. We do have an excellent account of this last fortnight of Mozart's life, but it comes from Constanze's sister, Sophie. It was in her arms, not Constanze's, that Wolfgang died. The story that Constanze threw herself on Mozart's bed when he died, in order to become infected, came years later from Constanze herself. No-one has corroborated it, and there is no other indication that Mozart's illness was infectious.

On April 7th 1825, Sophie wrote to Constanze's second husband, Georg Nissen, when he was writing his biography of Mozart. Constanze herself contributed no detail of any importance about her husband's death. Like Constanze, Sophie married a composer, Jakob Haibl, who was the choir-master at Diakovar, in Hungary.

This letter from Sophie is given in full as it describes so vividly the last few days of the composer, clearly remembered after thirty-four years:

Now I must tell you about Mozart's last days. Mozart became fonder and fonder of our dear departed mother and she of him. Indeed he often came running along in great haste to the Wieden [the district], where she and I were lodging at the Golden Plough, carrying under his arm a little bag containing coffee and sugar, which he would hand to our good mother, saying, 'Here, mother dear, now you can have a little *Jause* [afternoon drink].' She used to be as delighted as a child. He did this very often. In short, Mozart in the end never came to see us without bringing something.

When Mozart fell ill, we both made him a night-jacket which he could put on frontways, since on account of his swollen condition, he was unable to turn in bed. Then, as we did not know how seriously ill he was, we also made him a quilted dressing-gown. His dear wife, my sister, had given us the materials for both garments. We often visited him and he seemed to be really looking forward to wearing his dressing-gown. I used to go into town every day to see him. One Saturday when I was with him, Mozart said to me:

'Dear Sophie, do tell Mamma that I am fairly well, and that I shall be able to go and congratulate her on the octave [eighth day after her name-day].'

Who could have been more delighted than I to bring such cheerful news to my mother, who was always anxious to hear how he was? I hurried home to comfort her, the more so as he himself seemed to be bright and happy. The following day was a Sunday. I was young then and rather vain, I confess, and liked to dress up. But I never cared to go out walking from our suburb into town in my fine clothes, and I had no money for a drive. So I said to our good mother: 'Dear Mamma, I'm not going to see Mozart today. He was so well yesterday that surely he will be much better this morning, and one day more or less won't make much difference.' My mother said: 'Listen to this. Make me a cup of coffee, and then I'll tell you what you ought to do.'

She was inclined to keep me at home; and indeed my sister knows how much I had to be with her. I went into the kitchen. The fire was out. I had to light the lamp and make a fire. All the time I was thinking of Mozart. I had made the coffee and the lamp was still burning. Then I noticed how wasteful I had been with my lamp, I mean, that I had burned so much oil. It was still burning brightly. I stared into the flame and thought to myself, 'How I should love to know how Mozart is!' While I was thinking and gazing at the flame, it went out, as completely as if the lamp had never been burning. Not a spark remained on the main wick, and yet there was not the slightest draught – that I can swear to you.

A horrible feeling came over me. I ran to our mother and told her about all this. She said: 'Take off your fine clothes and go into town and bring me back news of him at once. But be sure not to delay!' I hurried along as fast as I could. How frightened I was when my sister, who was almost despairing and yet trying to keep calm, came out to me, saying; 'Thank God you have come! Last night he was so ill that I thought he would not be alive this morning. Do stay with me to-day, for if he has another bad turn, he will die tonight.' I tried to control myself and went to his bedside. He said: 'Ah, dear Sophie, how glad I am that you have come. You must stay here tonight and see me die.'

I tried hard to be brave and to persuade him to the contrary. But to all my attempts he only replied: 'Why, I am already tasting death. And, if you do not stay, who will support my dearest Constanze when I am gone?'

'Yes, yes, dear Mozart,' I assured him, 'but I must first go back to my mother and tell her that you would like me to stay with you today.'

'Yes, do so,' said Mozart, 'but be sure to come back soon.'

Good God, how distressed I felt! My poor sister followed me to the door and begged me for Heaven's sake to go to the priests at St Peter's and implore one of them to come to Mozart – a chance call, as it were – (as he had not asked for a priest himself). I did so, but for a long time they refused to come, and I had a great deal of trouble to persuade one of these holy brutes (*geistliche Unmenschen*) to stir. 'This musician has always been a bad Catholic,' one of the priests told me, 'I will not go to him.'*

Then I ran to my mother, who was anxiously waiting for me. It was already dark. Poor soul, how shocked she was! I persuaded her to go and spend the night with her eldest daughter, the late Josefa Hofer. I then ran back as fast as I could to my distracted sister. Süssmayr was at Mozart's bedside. The well-known Requiem lay on the quilt, and Mozart was explaining to him how, in his opinion, he ought to finish it when he was gone. Further, he urged his wife to keep his death a secret until she had informed Albrechtsberger, who was in charge of all the services [at St Stephens]. A long search was made for Dr Closset, who was found at the theatre, but who had to wait for the end of the play. He came and ordered cold poultices to be placed on Mozart's burning head, which, however, affected him to such an extent that he became unconscious and remained so until he died.

His last movement was an attempt to express with his mouth the drum passages in the Requiem. That I can still hear. Müller

* Schurig, *Mozart* (1922), p. 294. *Mozart–Album* (1856). p. 85.

from the Art Gallery came and took a cast of his pale, dead face. Words fail me, dearest brother, to describe how his devoted wife in her utter misery threw herself on her knees and implored the Almighty for his aid. She simply could not tear herself away from Mozart, however much I begged her to do so. If it was possible to increase her sorrow, this was done on the day after that distressing night, when crowds of people walked past the house and wept and mourned for him.

I have never seen Mozart irascible, still less furious. I simply cannot remember whether I told my sister about the light, an episode which was so striking in my opinion, because I always avoided most carefully reawakening her grief [literally, renewing her wound].

While Sophie was hurrying through the streets of Vienna, to St Peter's church to implore a priest to come to her brother-in-law before he died, and to tell her mother how ill he was, Mozart himself felt alert enough to take part in a bedside rehearsal of the Requiem. Benedikt Schack, who was taking the part of Tamino in the current performances of *The Magic Flute*, sang the soprano part, singing falsetto; Mozart sang the alto part; Franz Hofer, the violinist, sang the tenor, and the bass was sung by Franz Gerl, who was also in the cast of *The Magic Flute*, as Sarastro. As Sophie mentioned in her account of the last days of the composer, she had arranged for her mother to spend the night with her sister, Josefa, Hofer's wife, who, in Mozart's opera, was the Queen of the Night. The rehearsal began, and got as far as the *Dies Irae*, but, reaching the depiction of *lacrymosa dies illa* (*that tearful day*), Mozart had to stop singing and began to weep himself.

It cannot be stated definitely that the priests overcame their reluctance to visit Mozart on his death-bed. In her long and detailed letter Sophie is not precise on this point. He did not receive the last sacrament of extreme unction while he was alive; it was only given at the funeral service. The local priests had their own reasons for preferring not to visit the Mozart household. The Church was opposed to Freemasonry, and Mozart's membership of this organisation must have been known to them. But this would not have stopped a local priest coming to the bedside of a dying man, at the request of one of the family, unless there were further reasons, relating perhaps to his private life. If the priests knew anything relating to Mozart's feelings for Magdalena, and to Constanze's affection for Süssmayr, they may well have been reluctant to administer any sacrament in the Mozart apartment. And, it must be noted, Mozart himself never asked himself for a priest to come to his bedside.

After the performance at the theatre where Dr Closset was in attendance, he came to see his dying patient. Both he and Dr Matthias von Sallaba, who had also attended Mozart, were eminent physicians. Closset was the personal physician of the Emperor's Minister, Prince Wenzel von Kaunitz, and von Sallaba later became senior physician of the General Hospital in Vienna. Mozart could not have been in better hands. Closset, who had probably felt that there was nothing he could do, merely advised the application of a cold compress of vinegar and water to cool Mozart's head. As Sophie mentioned in her letter to Georg Nissen, she followed his instructions, but it had an adverse effect, shocking the dying man into a final state of unconsciousness. At five minutes to one, on the morning of Monday December 5th, Mozart died.

The cause of death was perhaps correctly diagnosed by Closset, but his report has never been published. There was no autopsy. In 1824, Dr Eduard Guldener wrote to Giuseppe Carpani, the author of a biography of Haydn, telling him that Dr Closset, from the beginning of Mozart's illness, 'feared a fatal conclusion, namely a deposit on the brain. Closset recognised the illness with such accuracy that he forecast its outcome almost to the hour. The statutory examination of the corpse did not reveal anything at all unusual. I shall have the greatest pleasure if this can contribute to giving the lie to the horrible calumny on the excellent Salieri.' The body may have been examined, but there is no record, no mention, of an autopsy, an investigation involving dissection. Guldener wanted to clear Salieri; and this honourable motive perhaps made him unduly keen to rule out the possibility of poison.

With only Mozart's symptoms and his previous medical history – one of recurrent rheumatic fever – on which to base their judgement, biographers of Mozart have put forward no less than ten different possible killers: uraemia, rheumatic fever, consumption, goitre, dropsy, Bright's Disease, mercury poisoning (as a result of the administration of mercury in medicines), miliary fever, inflammation of the brain and malignant typhoid fever.

If Mozart had shown symptoms which suggested all these possible causes, his two doctors must have been extremely confused, as we certainly are. The only cause stated on his death certificate was 'heated miliary fever'. This is clearly an evasion, as miliaria is simply an inflammation and swelling of the pores. It is caused by excessive sweating during a fever and produces a fine rash all over the body.

If each of the suggested causes of death is examined, it can be seen that they all contain one or more elements which conflict with the symptoms shown. The only known symptoms shown by Mozart were swelling of the body, inflammation of the joints, fever, headache and vomiting.

The actual cause of death may well have been uraemia, complicated by a terminal pneumonia. When a patient dies in a coma, as Mozart did, uraemia is one of the five causes first considered by a doctor – the others being apoplexy, epilepsy, injury and overdose or poison. Some of Mozart's symptoms indicate uraemia, such as vomiting and headaches, but the swelling of the joints indicates another cause. And when uraemia is the main cause of death, this usually comes after a slow, gradual decline often accompanied by drowsiness and fits, leading eventually to more prolonged coma. Mozart's death came quickly, after only a fortnight's illness, with a coma occurring only right at the end.

Inflammation of the joints, which become swollen, is one of the symptoms of rheumatic fever. This disease however usually starts with a streptococcal sore throat, which is followed two or three weeks later by more generalised symptoms. There is no record of Mozart complaining of a sore throat, and this particular illness came on suddenly. In an acute attack of this type of fever, death is rare, coming later with heart failure. Similarly death from consumption rarely occurs within three weeks. A sure sign of consumption is frequent coughing, with blood in the phlegm, and this was never mentioned by Sophie or anyone else who knew Mozart. Goitre seems a most unlikely cause of death, as swelling of the neck was not mentioned among the symptoms observed, and no-one commented on any pronounced nervousness and jumpiness, which are shown by sufferers from this complaint. Swelling is one of the symptoms of dropsy, but this is mainly of the legs, caused by back-pressure from a failing heart and engorgement of veins. Other symptoms shown by Mozart do not indicate heart failure as the main cause of death, and this is the basic factor of this illness. There is a possible connection between dropsy and a form of kidney disease, nephritis, which could be described as Bright's Disease. In cases of nephritis, a severe loss of protein is caused, and this can lead to dropsy. Bright's Disease is sometimes preceded by an acute sore throat, which is not one of the symptoms shown, as far as we know, by Mozart.

As mentioned above, 'heated miliary fever' tells us little, unless miliary tuberculosis is meant. Diagnosis of this form of tuberculosis is extremely difficult. If the lungs are affected, coughing and shortness of breath are prominent. If, on the other hand, the brain is affected – what would be described as inflammation of the brain – then headache and vomiting are two common symptoms, but convulsions are also caused. If Mozart had suffered in this way, Sophie and those who were with him during the last two days would have mentioned this. Photophobia, wishing to be in the dark, is another symptom. Mozart's desire to take part in a rehearsal of the Requiem during his last afternoon hardly indicates this tendency.

If he had been suffering from malignant typhoid fever, he would have been covered by the eruption of rose spots; and the patient usually becomes delirious. This is a highly contagious disease, one which would have caused Dr Closset to recommend isolation from Constanze and Sophie.

The only suggested cause of death not mentioned so far in this analysis is mercury poisoning. In chronic poisoning with this metal, tremors of the hands, increased salivation, irritability, shyness and deterioration of the personality are shown. Mozart, by all accounts, showed neither the physical nor mental symptoms, and maintained his courageous acceptance of death right to the end. However, two of the symptoms of mercury poisoning are vomiting and a metallic taste in the mouth. Mozart's reference to the taste of death, when he asked Sophie to stay with him to the end, indicates that there may have been some form of mercury or other poisoning. Here it must be pointed out that mercury poisoning may be confused, in a diagnosis, with uraemia, for this metal may damage the kidney and lead to a uraemic death.

The possibility of death by poison should not be ignored. Mozart himself not only thought that this *was* the cause of his death; he also thought he knew the type of poison used – aqua toffana. An examination of the component parts of this poison – white arsenic, antimony and lead oxide – is therefore necessary. In powdered or liquid form, it could easily be added to a glass of wine.

Symptoms shown by people who have swallowed arsenic include vomiting, cramp, nausea, loss of sensation in hands and feet, and weakness of the muscles of the limbs. The skin may become pigmented and occasionally show a vesicular rash. If this had been observed on Mozart's body, it might have been described – incorrectly – as a miliary rash, and this might be the reason for 'miliary fever' being mentioned as the cause of death in his death certificate. Some of the symptoms of arsenic poison given above were shown by Mozart.

Antimony is a flaky metallic substance, pale blue in colour, which is easily powdered. Like mercury, it can leave an unusual taste in the mouth and cause similar symptoms. The third ingredient of aqua toffana, lead oxide, would give rise to headaches, vomiting, paralysis of some muscles and a final coma. These poisons would not by themselves cause a fever, but this can occur as a terminal complication, as pneumonia. On December 31st 1791, a report written only a week after Mozart's death was included in a Berlin paper, *Musikalisches Wochenblatt*, saying that 'he died in Vienna at the end of last week. Because his body swelled up after death, some people believe that he was poisoned.'

If Mozart had been poisoned, his close friends may well have known the reasons why somebody wanted to kill him. If this involved some secrets relating to his private life, they would want to avoid all enquiries, and would do everything they could to keep public interest in his death to a minimum. The public would have to be informed where, officially, Mozart was buried, but the burial would have to take place quickly, before an autopsy could be carried out. Steps would also have to be taken to eliminate the possibility of an autopsy after exhumation. This would present many problems. All those involved would have to agree to remain silent when questioned about the burial. Government officials and the local priests would also have to agree.

If Mozart's friends decided on a form of burial which was in any degree shameful, Constanze, his widow, would also have to refrain from comment if the plan was to succeed. If she really loved Mozart and felt no bitterness about his affection for anyone else, it is surely most unlikely that she would consent to remain silent all her life about a disgraceful, anonymous burial for her own husband.

6

The Burial of Mozart
1791

SALIERI You are a God, though you may not believe it,
But I, I *know*. I have found a second Haydn,
Who brings me ecstasy and rapture.

MOZART Is it true, Salieri,
That Beaumarchais once poisoned someone?

Pushkin, MOZART AND SALIERI, *1830*

6

WE KNOW THE EXACT TIME of Mozart's death: five
minutes to one o'clock in the morning of December 5th
1791. But from now on we are plunged into darkness, doubts
and contradictions. Constanze is conspicuous, but only by her
absence and silence. It was Sophie, her sister, who looked after
Mozart as he lay dying; and it was in Sophie's arms, not
Constanze's, that he finally departed this life. While Sophie
described in some detail Mozart's last days, Constanze has told
us nothing. But neither sister has said a word about his burial.

Mozart's request that Albrechtsberger should be told of his
death at the earliest opportunity, so that he could apply
immediately for his post as assistant *Kapellmeister* at St
Stephen's cathedral, was complied with; and this application,
unlike Mozart's, was immediately accepted. Also informed of
Mozart's death early that morning was Baron Gottfried van
Swieten, at whose house Mozart had often played his compositions and taken part in recitals. This rich man was the Presi-
dent of the Commission for Education and Censorship. He
had befriended Mozart and had done much to foster his reputation. Without delay van Swieten came to the house and took
charge; Constanze, it seems, was not able to do so. He
arranged that she and her six-months-old baby should be
taken to stay with Joseph von Bauernfeld, a friend of
Schikaneder. For some reason or other, Constanze did not stay
long with Bauernfeld, and moved on to stay with Joseph
Goldhahn, the friend mentioned by Mozart in his letter to
Anton Stoll in June 1791 (chapter 3). What exactly was wrong
with Constanze, if there was any illness, we do not know for
certain.

Mozart's death had not come as a complete surprise. For the last week or so, his friends had probably seen that his last days had come. They had ample time to make a plan for his burial. As soon as van Swieten came on the scene, this plan was put into action. Constanze was taken to another part of the town; Joseph Deiner, the waiter from the 'Silver Snake', dressed the body of Mozart in an anonymous black burial garment; van Swieten made arrangements for the funeral service at St Stephen's cathedral. He arranged for the burial itself to take place, not at the main cemetery but at the graveyard of St Marx, on the outskirts of the town, two and a half miles from the cathedral. A humble, inconspicuous grave was ordered, which cost 8 gulden, 56 kreutzer; and 3 florins was put aside for the hearse.

At three o'clock on the following afternoon, December 6th, the brief funeral service began. It was held, not in the main body of the cathedral, but in a small vestibule, leading to the steps of the catacomb below. This vestibule is called the *Kapistrankapelle*, or the Crucifix Chapel of the new Vault. The public were not informed in advance; only a few friends would have been able to fit into this vestibule. Who attended the funeral service and who witnessed the burial? No-one is certain, but the following names have been recorded by Mozart's biographers, giving us at least a glimpse of those who were at the service at St Stephen's: Süssmayr, Roser, the conductor of the orchestra at Schikaneder's theatre, Orsler, the cellist, van Swieten, Deiner, Albrechtsberger, Mozart's two brothers-in-law, Lange and Hofer, and Antonio Salieri. Schikaneder may have been there also, perhaps with his brother Urban, who took the role of the First Priest in *The Magic Flute*. Also at the service may have been Anton Stadler, the clarinettist, Eybler, the composer, and Schack, the tenor. In his recent biography of Mozart, Arthur Hutchings quotes the historian, Erich Schenk,* stating that 'several Freemasons, van Swieten and other members of the nobility were present' at the funeral service. Constanze did not attend the service or the burial.

* Erich Schenk, *Mozart and His Times* (1960) p. 447.

Who accompanied the hearse to the cemetery is not known. What is known is that Mozart was not buried in the grave that would have cost 8 gulden, 56 kreutzer. His coffin was lowered, we are told, into a communal grave that was left unmarked – a burial for which no money was required.

In other words there is no evidence at all that Mozart was indeed buried in this graveyard. He might have been buried anywhere. If traces of poison had been found in the body, they would have been easily discovered in an autopsy. In the Register of Deaths of St Stephen's, December 6th is given as the date of burial, but there is some doubt as to whether it occurred on the Tuesday or the Wednesday, December 7th.

A determined concealment of the facts was now undertaken by all concerned. This has caused subsequent writers on this subject to indulge in a variety of inadequate explanations, feeble evasions and patent inaccuracies. Constanze's second husband, Georg Nissen, in his biography of Mozart, might have been expected to shed some light on this shameful treatment of his revered subject. But all he has to say about Mozart's burial is this: 'Swieten took care of the burial of Mozart's body, and because he took into account the greatest economy for the family, the coffin was lowered into a common grave and every other expense was avoided.'

Sacheverell Sitwell, in his biography of Mozart, wrote these words: 'No-one troubled to give him an expensive burial, and, as it rained violently, the few friends who were there hurried home. The coffin was put hastily in a pauper's grave and covered over. A few weeks later all trace of it had been lost among the coffins of the other paupers; and to this day, the body has never been found.'

Mozart was *not* a pauper. It is inconceivable that his friends, who had taken the trouble to attend the funeral service, would allow him to be dumped in an unmarked, communal grave – unless they had all agreed to this beforehand. It is absurd to pretend that stormy weather would make devoted friends abandon the coffin before it was decently buried. There was, in fact, no storm. Count Karl Zinzendorf tells us in his diary that on the day of the funeral the weather in Vienna was 'mild, with frequent mist'. This is confirmed by the official barometric readings and the general weather report. Who lied about the storm in the first place? Why was such a story concocted? It could only have been made up in order to explain away the anonymous disposal of the corpse.

W. J. Turner, in his biography, gives this surprising explanation: 'The wealthy Baron van Swieten made all the funeral arrangements. As if inspired by God, he arranged for the cheapest burial possible (third-class).'

Mozart was not given a third-class burial. He was given the type of burial for which no payment is required. Turner goes on to add this equally odd piece of information: 'No grave was bought and nobody was present when the corpse of Mozart was flung into a common pauper's vault containing fifteen to twenty coffins.'

This is an amazing collection of untruths and confusing statements. The author, evidently, knows that no-one was around when the body was somehow lowered into the ground; and, although no-one knows where the body was placed, it is known roughly how many other bodies were dumped there. Finally it was not placed in a vault but a pit. But perhaps it was not taken there at all.

In 1856 'an ordinary man' who had been 'in personal contact' with Mozart, in Otto Jahn's opinion, Joseph Deiner, published a brief Memoir. In it he wrote that 'only a few friends and three women accompanied the corpse. Mozart's wife was not present'. [Deutsch, p. 565] One of the women was probably Sophie.

The most comprehensive collection of data about Mozart's life is Otto Deutsch's *Mozart, a Documentary Biography* (1956). Here we are told by Deutsch that 'It was not a pauper's funeral, but the cheapest available. That neither the widow nor close friends, nor yet any of the freemasons attended the procession is explicable only by the simplicity that became customary in Emperor Joseph's time.'

If it was not a pauper's funeral, why was Mozart thrown

into a pauper's communal grave? Why say that his close friends did not accompany the coffin to the cemetery? If that is indeed true, then it is most significant. If Mozart was not buried in the cemetery of St Marx, then it is quite understandable that none of his friends went there. Hermine Cloeter, in her book on Mozart's burial, *Die Grabstätte W. A. Mozarts* (Vienna, 1956) tells us that none of the composer's friends witnessed this final act. But she says that 'The gravedigger was instructed to lower the coffin into a burial pit. [His friends] let the hearse continue its gloomy journey alone.'

The reason given for this indifference is the already discredited stormy weather. Deutsch's reference to 'the simplicity' of burials in Joseph's time is also an inadequate explanation. Trying to give this evasion more substance, two recent biographies of Mozart offer this information: 'On August 23, 1784, Joseph II made burial in church crypts illegal. It was decreed that the dead should not be buried in coffins but merely sewn into sacks and covered with quicklime before being interred. It is true that he had to repeal the law after a riot against its enforcement had led to bloodshed.' [Arthur Hutchings, *Mozart, the Man, the Music*, 1976]

And Hugh Ottoway in *Mozart* (1979) writes: 'It was not an age of sumptuous burials. Indeed, during the Josephine era, such "superstitious" practices were actively discouraged; for a time it was decreed that coffins be abandoned in favour of sacks and quicklime, and a number of ceremonies were abolished.'

Aware, perhaps, of the vagueness of this excuse for the anonymous disposal of Mozart's body, this author adds a quotation from another recent work, in which all the details given may be pure fiction, as they lack any authenticity: 'The blast of wind and sleet made the few mourners turn back at the city gate and leave the light coffin on the hearse to hired men, to a priest at the graveside and to a gravedigger.' [Ilsa Barea, *Vienna, Legend and Reality*, 1966]

Not one of Mozart's biographers, however, has mentioned any other Austrian, famous or obscure, who was buried in this unorthodox manner. Joseph's decree of 1784 was rescinded in the following year, six years before Mozart died. It discouraged the use of coffins; but we know that Wolfgang *was* put in a coffin; and there was nothing in this decree which forbade burial in single, marked graves in graveyards. It stipulated that 'all corpses must be laid out in a linen sack without clothes in a coffer [*Truhe*] and so be brought to the cemetery. There they are to be covered with unslaked lime and buried in the earth on the same day.'

When carrying out this kind of burial, priests made use of coffins, the bottoms of which had been specially prepared. When the coffin was lowered into the grave, a short pull on a rope opened the bottom; the body fell through it, and the coffin was lifted up again. This ruling caused such hostility that on January 20th 1785, it was decreed that this new type of burial was no longer compulsory. No biographer of Mozart has pointed out that other composers and relatives of Mozart were buried at this time in the usual manner. Dittersdorf, for example, in 1799, Michael Haydn in 1806, Leopold Mozart in 1787, Constanze's mother in 1793, and her aunt, Genoveva Weber, in 1797, were all buried in the usual Christian fashion.

Yet another weak and muddled explanation is given by the only book published in recent years on Mozart's death and burial, *Mozart: Krankheit, Tod, Begräbnis*, 1966, by C. Bär. This short work ends with this concluding paragraph: 'For posterity, which has another attitude to death and burial, it is a misfortune that Mozart died so young. If he had lived another ten years, he would probably have found enough fame to have ensured a state funeral and a single grave, like Gluck before him and Haydn after him. But his death occurred at a time which was averse to that kind of grave cult, but also Mozart's greatness was not fully appreciated.'

This suggestion that Mozart was buried as a pauper without a name partly because he was still unappreciated by the Viennese is absurd, and an insult to his contemporaries. Two days after his death, on December 7th 1791, the *Wiener Zeitung* used these superlative terms to describe his genius: 'In the night of

December 4th and 5th of this month, there died the *Hofkammerkompositeur* Wolfgang Mozart. Known from his childhood as the possessor of the finest musical talent in all Europe, through the fortunate development of his exceptional natural gifts and through persistent application, he climbed to the pinnacle of the greatest Masters.'

The Magic Flute was being performed to full houses in the National Theatre (as mentioned in Mozart's letters of October 7th, 9th, and 14th 1791); and as soon as the Viennese heard of his death, they gathered outside his house, as Sophie Haibl pointed out in her letter to Constanze's second husband.

The fact cannot be denied that Mozart, as a composer, lived at an ideal time and in the ideal city. Vienna was then the musical capital of the world. He was not a lonely man, with no friends to ensure that he was given a decent Christian burial, with no widow to protect his honour and good name. Taken by itself, Constanze's absence at the funeral service is not surprising, as widows and other female relatives often remained at home. But her conduct after Mozart's death is clearly and consistently shameful. She made no effort to visit St Marx' graveyard for seventeen years, finally going there at the request of her second husband, Georg Nissen. In Sophie's letter to Nissen, already quoted, she mentioned the visit of Josef Müller, from the Art Gallery, who made a death-mask of the composer in the morning of December 5th. Müller, whose real name was Count Josef Deym, owned a wax-work collection in Vienna. The original mask disappeared, but a copy was made and given to Constanze. This would, one would imagine, be a treasured possession. Unlike so many details concerning Mozart after his death which we would like to know, we do know that Constanze smashed this last image of her first husband – and we know what she said on this occasion. She was 'glad that the ugly old thing was broken'.*

If Constanze had the slightest objection to the manner in which Mozart was finally disposed of, she could have forbid-

* *Letters of Mozart*, Anderson edition, p. 1450. S. A. Schurig, *Leopold Mozarts Reiseaufzeichnungen*, p. 92.

den it. She could have left, at a later date, some record of her disgust. She had, it seems, no criticism to make of a communal burial pit as Wolfgang's last resting place. A further disturbing act of indifference occurred when, a day or two after Mozart's death, Joseph Deiner came to see her and implored her to put a cross, or some mark, on the communal grave. She refused, saying, 'Let the church do it!' The clergy themselves likewise refused, so nothing was done.

Van Swieten's arrangements were carried out smoothly; not one of those who attended the funeral service divulged any further detail about this tragic conclusion of Mozart's life. A further fact, relating to the career of van Swieten, concerns the termination of his office as Minister for Education. Officially he ceased to be a member of the government on December 5th 1791, the same day as Mozart's death. This could, admittedly, be pure coincidence; on the other hand, there was the possibility that his arrangements on behalf of Constanze for the burial of her husband, might have gone awry, and that embarrassing questions might have been asked – with, perhaps, scandalous revelations. If this had happened, it could then be stated that, when Mozart was buried, van Swieten was not officially connected with the government.

We know the names of the other people buried in this cemetery on and around December 6th – men and women who were lowered into single, marked graves; they are all without renown. Every seven years the communal burial pits were cleared out; the bones of the dead were broken up and thrown away. This is the last, physical detail in the story of Mozart's body.

According to Hermine Cloeter, in her book on Mozart's burial, *Die Grabstätte W. A. Mozarts*, it was the gravedigger who first told Constanze that she ought to place a cross over her husband's grave. Here at last we have someone who knew where Mozart lay. When someone later went to the graveyard to question the gravedigger, he found that a new man had been given the job. The man he had replaced could not be found. Constanze, as already mentioned, refused to do anything, saying that it was up to the vicar to erect a cross over the grave. Joseph Deiner also tried to persuade her to carry out this simple task, but he, according to Cloeter, 'got short shrift from her'. In other words, she was not merely uncooperative; she was offensive.

> Many a bitter word may have been passed about this [she writes]. Mozart's grave was devoid of any sign of commemoration and love – no stone, no cross, no name, no flowers – untraceable! Quite apart from any emotional judgement of her behaviour, the confusion which Constanze caused was – and has remained – wicked [*heillos*]. Later, she repeatedly declared that she thought that 'the vicar arranges to get the cross himself'. It did not occur to her to check whether this really had been done. She was never drawn to visit the burial place of the man who blessed her with his glorious name, who loved her most tenderly. She never felt obliged to show her sons the last resting place of their father. Seventeen years had to pass before she – at the instigation of others – went to have a look at her husband's grave, which already had the reputation of being untraceable. Constanze's lovelessness and impiety, which failed to observe the most simple and most natural duty – soon aroused people's displeasure.

This conduct shows not merely indifference. Her refusal even to go through the motions of gratitude and love indicates, surely, positive antipathy, if not ill will. In the short biographical study of Constanze by Arthur Schurig (1922) – the only one of its kind – the author declares that 'one is hardly wrong in saying that, had Mozart not reached his subsequent fame, Constanze would have very quickly forgotten him altogether.' If her love for Mozart had become so minimal, it would not have been in any way surprising if she had turned her attention towards another man. In his summing-up of her character, Schurig found her 'petty, vain, greedy, primitive, ... with a strongly developed element of self-love'. On the other hand, she was, in his opinion, 'a vivacious, good-natured creature'.

In 1805 Haydn expressed his disgust at her refusal to honour Mozart. In this year a conversation of his was reported in which he said: 'Despite the many years which have elapsed since he departed from us, Mozart's grave is still not marked with any sign. It would be a crying shame if posterity were not to know the spot where his mortal remains were laid. This really pains my heart. I still hope that something will be done, nevertheless, and that it will be carried out by the people whose responsibility it really is.'

7

Magdalena
1791–92

PAMINA This dagger will be my bridegroom. Patience, my
darling, I am yours. Soon we will be united!

THE MAGIC FLUTE *1791*

ONLY A FEW MINUTES' WALK away from St Stephen's cathedral in Vienna is the Grünangergasse, the street in which Magdalena Hofdemel lived with her husband, Franz. He, and possibly Magdalena herself, might have been among the small group of friends who attended Mozart's funeral service at the church on the afternoon of December 6th. Some historians state that a few of the composer's Masonic friends came to this service, and one of them could well have been Hofdemel. However, if he did attend, his name was never mentioned as one of the gathering. After the service Mozart's body, as we have seen, was removed from the church – and from sight – and buried in such a way that no-one could be certain where it was.

Had Mozart died a natural death, there would have been no reason for the ignominious burial in an unmarked grave. But if he were poisoned, if this were the reason for his rapid burial, who was the murderer? Apart from Salieri's senile ravings, there is no proof that he was involved. However, the day after Mozart's death, an extraordinary event happened which is worth examining in detail.

The Hofdemels lived in an apartment on the first floor of no. 10 Grünangergasse. During the day of December 6th a man came to the ground floor flat to carry out work of some kind. He heard a loud exchange of words coming from the flat upstairs, and this was followed by screams and a loud shriek. He took no action, perhaps because such bitter scenes were sadly frequent in the Hofdemel household. Some time later a visitor to the flat on the first floor, unable to gain admittance, decided to break in, having heard perhaps that there had been an altercation which ended in screams. A locksmith was summoned; the door to the apartment had to be lifted off its hinges and the lock broken. Fearing that some criminal act of violence had been committed, the visitor took with him two witnesses.

Their worst fears were confirmed. Magdalena was lying in a pool of blood, slashed across the face, neck, shoulder and arms. The next room was also locked and had to be broken into. There lay Hofdemel. His throat was cut; a razor still lay in his hand. A local physician, Dr Gunther, was told of the tragedy; he came at once and found that Magdalena was still alive. Her wounds were washed and bound, smelling salts were applied, and air was pumped into her lungs with a pair of bellows. At last she revived. Dr Gunther and a surgeon, Dr Rossman, did everything they could to save Magdalena. She was in the fifth month of pregnancy.*

Hofdemel's body should have been sewn into a cow's skin and thrown into an unmarked pit by the hangman, for this was the official burial for those who had killed themselves. The corpse was examined by a surgeon, Johann Christian Sartori, who spared Magdalena this shameful burial of her husband. He was buried in an unmarked, unknown grave on December 10th. In the official government press archives, December 6th is given as the date of his death. Possibly to discourage anyone linking this death with that of Mozart, the *Wiener Zeitung* incorrectly stated that Hofdemel had died on December 10th, the day of his burial. The cover-up had begun.

There were, however, two people who would be able to confirm or deny the rumours which were now spreading in the capital about the tragic end of Mozart's love of Magdalena – Constanze and Magdalena herself. This was, in fact, a situation in which silence can be regarded as confirmation, as both parties would be only too glad to deny the rumours if they were false.

Otto Jahn, in his four-volume biography which appeared in

* Dr Ernst Weizmann, *Die Weltpresse* (1956), February 4th–April 28th 1956. Otto Deutsch, Mozart, *A Documentary Biography* (1965), pp. 418, 426.

the centenary year of 1856, briefly mentioned Mozart's affair with Magdalena without going into details, but this was only included in the first edition.* Jahn was given the full story about Magdalena by Ludwig von Köchel, the musicologist, whose reliability in all other matters has not been doubted. Another source of information was Karl Czerny. It was at the house of Czerny's parents that Magdalena Hofdemel stayed whenever she came to Vienna from her father's house in Brünn, where she lived after her husband's suicide. In Jahn's *Collected Essays on Music* (1866) he declared that 'it seems to me totally unjustified to doubt the reliability of Czerny's informa-tion.'† While he accepted the veracity of this information, Jahn did not divulge the true story in any detail, thinking, one must suppose, that it would harm Mozart's reputation.

In the brief reports about Hofdemel's suicide in the Austrian *provincial* papers, the marks of censorship are clearly evident, both in the wording of these reports and in absence of com-ment in the *Viennese* journals. What is apparent is the import-ance attached to this suicide by members of the Court, and the sympathy accorded to Magdalena by the highest in the land. This, combined with the brevity of the announcements in the press, indicates unmistakably that, in the eyes of the govern-ment and the aristocracy, a ghastly tragedy had occurred which involved someone of the greatest importance. When a genius of the first rank dies, his work is no longer taken for granted, and anyone who was near and dear to him is more likely to be shown great sympathy and respect.

The first paper to report the news was the *Pressburger Zeitung*. On December 7th it merely stated that a man had committed suicide after having tried to commit murder. No name was given. Then, a week later, on December 13th, the *Grätzer Zeitung* revealed that 'jealousy and other domestic circumstances caused rows and anger' between Frau and Herr Hofdemel, 'who has committed suicide'. Two days later the story was repeated in the same paper, but this time it was stated

* Jahn, Vol. 3, pp. 175, 179, 230.
† *Allgemeine Musikzeitung* (1863), p. 171.

that 'it is known that faint-heartedness [*Kleinmut*] was the reason for the attempted murder of Frau Hofdemel and the suicide of Hofdemel himself.' This time details were added which must have aroused the readers' curiosity. 'Not only many women, but even Her Majesty the Empress herself, have promised support to this woman, whose conduct they know is blameless.' A third report on the suicide appeared in the same newspaper on December 20th. This time the readers were told that 'Hofdemel explained to his wife that he wanted to die and asked her whether she wanted to go with him. The suicide was an act of jealousy, of the most wretched passion.' The name of her lover was omitted.

On the following day, December 21st, the readers of the *Pressburger Zeitung* were given a few further details of the tragedy, and, by its wording, invited to make their own conclusions. 'The widow of the suicide who, as is now known, took his life from dejection rather than jealousy, is still alive, and not only several ladies, but also Her Majesty the Empress herself, have promised assistance to this woman, whose conduct is known to be unexceptionable. Provision has also been made for the widow of the late *Kapellmeister* Mozart. His Majesty the Emperor has granted her her husband's full salary, and Baron van Swieten has provided for her son.'

On January 6th 1792, the *Grätzer Burgerzeitung* told its readers that 'Frau Hofdemel is now out of all danger and can already speak again. She will, however, by no means admit the cause of this ghastly event, and is satisfied merely to say that she loved her husband and will never cease to mourn his death sincerely.' No reference would be made, in other words, either to the smoke or the fire. And in the following month, on February 9th, the *Grätzer Zeitung* returned to the Hofdemel suicide, and stated that

Frau Hofdemel, who was so badly treated by her husband, who began raving so suddenly, is now, through the skill and tireless work of Doctors Peter Rossman and Gunther, already restored to health again, to the extent that she can convey her thanks

personally to the highest in the land and to other members of
the nobility. [*den höchsten und hohen Herrschaften*] The degree to
which the fate of this most unfortunate woman has stirred the
sympathy of almost everybody is now so well known that I do
not need to report on it. Our great Empress herself enquired
about the condition of Frau Hofdemel, promised her comfort
and soothed her pains by the most gracious announcement that
the Emperor will take care of the future welfare of this woman.
Many noble friends comfort her, amongst them most notably
the Countess von Stahremberg and the Countess von Chotek.

Early in 1792 the readers of the *Vienna Journal for Ladies**
were told that a man who lived in the same house as the
Hofdemels 'heard Hofdemel shout: "It's the end for me!
There's no help any more. I must die!" Hofdemel attacked his
wife with a razor and seriously wounded her, shouting:
"Woman, no-one else will have you! You must die with me!"'
The way in which Hofdemel tried to kill his wife, attempting
to disfigure her and destroy her beauty are typical of a murderer prompted by jealousy.

When this attack occurred, Magdalena's one-year-old
daughter, Therese, may have been in the apartment. It may
have been her cries that finally brought about Magdalena's
rescue. After her father's death, a friend of the family, Lorenz
Weiss, a Court official, was made Therese's guardian.

Only one letter written by Magdalena has so far come to
light. It is undated, but it seems as if it must have been composed in March 1792, some three months after her husband's
suicide. Taking into account what is, and is not, said in this
letter, one can deduce that it was written with the help of an
officially appointed solicitor.

Honourable Magistrate of the Royal City of Vienna,
    It is unfortunately too well known in what kind of wretched,
miserable condition my husband, Herr Franz Hofdemel, chancery clerk of the esteemed High Court, placed me, with many
wounds on my face and also on parts of my body, which has
ruined my health and which perhaps may well do so for the rest

* 1792, no. 2, p. 37.

of my life. He has left me in this condition as the mother of one child and another still to be hoped for. His whole estate would not be sufficient to compensate me for all this, and I am so convinced of the justice and fairness of the honourable State Magistrate that I believe, were I to request various things, they would be granted to me.

My request is that as a compensation 1,000 gulden be allowed me, to be paid out of the legacy – to cover the cost of raising another child, the numerous expenses, specified below, incurred during my ill-health, some of which have not yet been settled, and my widow's pension, and that this should respectively be kept liquid, as a claim on the legacy. The expenses mentioned above consist of the following:

	Gulden	Kreutzer
Dr Peter Rossman	55	90
Frau von Braun, for attendance	25	
Dr Franz Xaver Gunther	40	30
Chemist	11	50
Treasury official	3	10
Shoemaker	4	12
Tailor	28	37
Carpenter, for repairing the front door	1	45
Locksmith		45
Glazier		54
Painter	1	30
Builder		24
Hairdresser	9	
Chambermaid, for three months and bread money	9	
Laundry maid, for three months	7	
Coachman, for necessary visits	3	06
Supply of fire wood	11	47
Domestic expenses, from December 7th to March 17th 1792	163	22½
Total	374	42½

May it please you, Honourable Magistrate, to grant the above mentioned 1,000 gulden, in consideration of the amount

of the Franz Hofdemel legacy, and to keep it in cash as arranged
to this end, in consultation with the children's guardian, Court
Agent von Hörlein, before the impending holiday, as I must
soon leave for Brünn, to stay with my family, on account of the
late stage of my pregnancy. I shall stay in Brünn.

Magdalena Hofdemel*

The dates given for the last item on Magdalena's list of
expenses confirm that the suicide of her husband occurred on
December 6th, and that the letter may have been written on, or
soon after, March 17th. She did not have long to wait for a
reply. Four days later, on March 21st, she was given the
necessary authority, a power of attorney, to apply to the Royal
and High Court Advocate and Public Notary, Johann Sigis-
mund Rizy. On April 6th, a fortnight later, all the parties
concerned met and discussed her application. At this meeting
it was decided to give Magdalena the sum of 560 gulden.

One might have expected that certain items on the list
would be queried, such as the inclusion of bills for a shoemaker
and a tailor, for someone who had been bed-ridden for some of
the time since the attack on her life. The officials might have
queried the 163 gulden for unspecified 'domestic expenses'. In
the event, all the items listed were accepted. Magdalena left the
capital and returned to her father's house in Brünn, a day's
coach ride away, having made it clear in her formal application
to the Magistrate that she would do this. Among the various
possessions claimed, as her own property, was the pianoforte,
on which she had played Mozart's music at her private recitals.

Her son was baptised in Brünn on May 10th by the Royal
Appellation Chancellor, Johann von Nepomuk Alexander
Fidel Holderer. The baby was christened Johann von
Nepomuk Alexander Franz, the names of the godfather and of
Hofdemel himself.

Magdalena's father, Gotthard Pokorny, died in Brünn on
August 4th 1802. Her son, Johann, died, it is assumed, before
August 1804. On August 2nd of that year the interest on the

* Vienna State Archives no. 1,059 ex. 1,792.

inherited capital was made over entirely to Therese, and his name is not mentioned in the records again.

From time to time Magdalena visited Vienna and stayed with the Czernys. Karl, their son, was being given piano lessons by Beethoven, and Magdalena, on one visit, asked Czerny if she could hear him play some of his music. Czerny went to see Beethoven himself, when his son was having a lesson, and told him about Magdalena's request. 'Hofdemel?' enquired Beethoven, 'Isn't that the woman who had the affair with Mozart?' Czerny told him that it was indeed Magdalena. On hearing this, Beethoven said that he would never play in front of her. He was, however, persuaded later on to change his mind and play for her. Otto Jahn was told about this interesting episode by Karl Czerny, when he was staying in Vienna in 1852.*

This episode is doubly revealing. Beethoven's question and Czerny's reply show that both men knew of the affair, and Beethoven's embittered reaction indicates that he considered that this affair led to Mozart's death. If there was no connection, if jealousy had been the only reason for Hofdemel's attempt to kill Magdalena and for his suicide, then Beethoven could not have held her in any way responsible for Mozart's death. If Mozart was poisoned by Hofdemel, then indeed there would be a direct link between Magdalena and the death of Wolfgang.

On August 19th 1827, Karl Friedrich Zelter, builder and composer of songs, wrote to Goethe, whom he knew well and with whom he corresponded frequently. In this letter he referred to Mozart's private life, in a way that would never be suspected by those who have read only conventional biographies of the *maestro*: 'We remember the circumstances of Mozart's death only too well. As a result of such good training, production went so smoothly that he had time for a hundred things, time which he spent with women; in consequence it did not do him any good.'

The story of Mozart's love of Magdalena, with many

---

* Otto Jahn, *Gesammelte Aufsätze* (Leipzig, 1886) p. 330.

fictional details, next appeared in a novella by Leopold Schefer in 1841, fifty years after the composer's death. In his introduction Schefer said this about the truth of this romance and its tragic end: 'Since the newspapers have made public this true episode, and since the Germans, like the Greeks and the Italians, call for a true account of the lives of their artists, so this moving story will, I hope, be regarded as a useful contribution.'

In writing this novella, Schefer was supported and encouraged by his patron, Prince von Puchler-Muskau. In assembling facts about Mozart for his biography of Mozart, Otto Jahn found Schefer's account of value. Once again, in 1874, the Viennese were reminded of the affair by the publication of *Wolfgang and Constanze*, a short play with music by Franz von Suppé, the Italian composer who spent nearly all his life in Vienna. On page 7, we are asked: 'Does one not know that Mozart had an affair with a woman whose husband cut his own throat?'

In the only book written on Constanze herself, a short biographical study by Arthur Schurig, published in Dresden in 1922, the author, who had already written a full-length biography of Mozart, makes a surprising admission. In the text of the book he does not mention Mozart's love of Magdalena, but in the index he mentions Magdalena in these terms: 'p. 43. Hofdemel, Magdalena, friend and lover [*Geliebte*] of Mozart.'

On page 43 the author merely names Franz and Magdalena Hofdemel, among others, as friends of Mozart, and, a few pages later, Hofdemel's suicide is pushed into the background with the laconic statement that after Mozart's death one of his admirers [*Gläubige*] 'tried to kill himself.'

The fullest treatment of Hofdemel's jealousy and of the attempted murder of Magdalena has been given in *Franz Hofdemel*, a novella by Wolfgang Goetz, published in Vienna in 1932. In this work the author demonstrates lucidly how easily a responsible, rational man can deteriorate into a murderer, goaded, as Hofdemel was, by his beautiful wife's preference for a man whose genius made him feel inferior and a failure. Beauty and genius have this in common: both disturb the most rational of men. Hofdemel, a conscientious civil servant, holding a responsible position, found himself confronted with both these self-evident signs of excellence. No portrait of Magdalena has come to light. In view of her beauty, which the newspapers remarked on, it is unlikely that no artist painted her. Like so much that has been destroyed, which sheds light upon her, any likeness of her seems to have perished.

Goetz, in this work, draws our attention to the libretto of *The Magic Flute*. On the night before Hofdemel's savage attack and his own suicide, he and Magdalena go to a performance of this opera.* Over and over again the words uttered on stage startle him with their relevance to his own disturbed state of mind, to his own situation. He even identifies with Monostatos, the Moor, who is spurned by Pamina:

> Every being feels love's pleasure,
> Fondles, dallies, hugs and kisses;
> Am I thus to be avoided
> Just because my face is black?
> Is it that I have no heart?
> Am I not of flesh and blood?

Hofdemel hears the Queen of the Night proclaim that

> Hellish vengeance burns within me;
> Death and despair have now inflamed me!

In this opera the Three Spirits declare that 'Suicide is a sin against God in you'; and for committing this sin Hofdemel was buried without a name in an unknown place. Mozart, as Goetz reminds us in his novella, loved to sing Papageno's arias, and it is possible that when he wrote music for Papagena, he was thinking of Magdalena Pokorny (the name is pronounced Pakorny), as she was before her marriage. Mozart loved to

---

* In fact, as a mark of respect, there were no performances of the opera during Mozart's final illness, clear evidence of his renown.

make up names for his friends; he called himself 'Punkitititi' and Constanze 'SchablaPumfa', in a letter to Gottfried Jacquin, in 1787.

PAPAGENO	Is she young?
PRIEST	Young and beautiful
PAPAGENO	And she's called?
PRIEST	Papagena!...

THREE SPIRITS Now Papageno, look around!
Papageno turns round and sees her

PAPAGENO	Pa-pa-pa-Papagena!
PAPAGENA	Pa-pa-pa-Papageno!
PAPAGENO	Are you now wholly mine?
PAPAGENA	Now I am wholly yours!
PAPAGENO	Now you are my darling wife!
PAPAGENA	Now you are my little dove!

In an earlier scene Papagena appears disguised as an ugly old woman. Papageno asks if she has a lover. 'Of course I have!' she replies. He then asks, 'Is he as young as you?' Her reply is that her lover is ten years older, and that his name is Papageno. Mozart was ten years older than Magdalena. The opera ends with a triumphant hymn of praise to Isis and Osiris. The music for the final lines of the Chorus may well have been composed with Magdalena and Mozart himself in mind:

CHORUS The Powerful Ones [Isis and Osiris] have conquered.
Beauty and Wisdom are rewarded with an everlasting crown.

It is unlikely that Hofdemel remained in ignorance of his wife's love of Mozart until the day he attacked her and killed himself. What triggered off this sudden outburst of passion, evidently, was Mozart's death. If Hofdemel had not poisoned him, if he had played no part in his death, he surely would have felt glad that Magdalena's lover would no longer humiliate him or endanger his marriage. If he was overcome by guilt, remorse and terror, fearing imminent discovery of his crime, such feelings could easily have driven him to terminate the whole ghastly tragedy by attempting to kill Magdalena, her unborn child and finally himself. He nearly succeeded in achieving all three deaths. He made no effort to kill their little daughter, Therese, who was probably in another room in the flat. She was only a year old, too young to tell anyone about her father's crime.

But Magdalena survived. Not surprisingly she refused to divulge what happened the day after Mozart died.

8

Constanze
1791–1842

8

ON THE BACK of a page in Mozart's album, on which he had recorded, four years earlier, his grief at the death of his friend and doctor, Siegmund Barisani, Constanze wrote the following tribute to her husband:

> What you once wrote to your friend on this page, I now in my affliction write to you, dearly beloved husband; Mozart – never to be forgotten by me or by the whole of Europe – now you too are at peace – eternal peace!! About one o'clock in the morning of the 5th December in this year he left in his 36th year – alas! all too soon! – this good – but ungrateful world! – dear God! – For 8 years we were joined together by the most tender bond, never to be broken here below! – O! could I soon be joined with you for ever,
>
> Your grievously afflicted wife
Constanze Mozart née Weber

It has been doubted whether Constanze really wrote this on December 5th 1791, the day of Wolfgang's death, in spite of the fact that she added this date at the end of this inscription. The tone seems forced and unspontaneous. 'Never to be forgotten by the whole of Europe' sounds an unlikely remark for Constanze to make at a moment when, she would have us believe, she was prostrate and distraught with grief. She had, in fact, been married to Mozart for nine years.

Only five days after the funeral Constanze had an audience with the Emperor himself. At this meeting she submitted a written application for a pension, and assured Leopold that, with a sum of 3,000 gulden, she could settle all her husband's debts. In fact his debts amounted to no more than 1,000 gulden. Nothing could be simpler: the Emperor told Constanze that a benefit concert in Vienna would solve the problem, and he himself made such an event unnecessary by giving her enough money to pay off all the money owed. And she was awarded a pension of 266 gulden a year. But a benefit concert on December 28th, organised by Baron van Swieten, brought in more money.

The wording of Constanze's petition for a pension is interesting, as it confirms that, when Mozart died, his prospects were rapidly improving. There is no suggestion that he died worn out by depression and neglect.

Your Majesty!

The undersigned has had the misfortune to suffer the irreparable loss of her husband, and to be left by him with two infant sons, in circumstances which border upon indigence and want.

She knows, to her still greater distress, that because her deceased husband had not yet completed ten years' service, according to the existing qualification for a pension, she has no claim whatsoever to any allowance, and that there is therefore no course left to her but to trust in Your Majesty's favour and well-known love of providing for the indigent of all kinds.

But, lest she might perhaps appear unworthy of your most gracious benevolence, she ventures humbly to present a feeble description of her most unhappy plight and of its causes:

1 Her late husband never had the good fortune here in Vienna to meet with the propitious opportunity that would have allowed him to reveal his talents sufficiently to begin to improve his prospects in the world – and it was for that reason that he was not in a position to leave any means. It would moreover in the

2nd place have gone very easily with him abroad to make his fortune and to place his family in more brilliant circumstances, had he given heed to frequent propositions, and not chosen to seek his greatest fame in the favour of this most illustrious Court.

3rdly, granted that he was still in the prime of life and had the most likely prospect of being able to establish the well-being of his dependants in good time through his rare talent, it will be seen that there was no room in his thoughts for the possibility of the present situation.

Hence it came about that he never thought to ensure provision, however meagre, for his dependants by enrolling them in the Society for the Widows and Orphans of Musicians.

4thly. Finally this picture is the more pitiful in that he was snatched from the world at that very moment when his prospects for the future were beginning to grow brighter on all sides. Besides the reversion which he recently obtained of the position of *Kapellmeister* at St Stephen's Cathedral, he was assured shortly before his death of an annual subscription of 1,000 gulden from a number of the Hungarian nobility; while from Amsterdam he was advised of a still larger annual sum, for which he would have had to compose only a few works for the exclusive use of the subscribers.

The petitioner presumes to commend herself once more to your gracious favour and well-known paternal benevolence, especially towards cases of need of this kind, all the more completely in that only one thing still suffices to support her in her grievous situation, namely her confidence that Your Majesty will not exclude her and her *two infant sons* from your gracious liberality.

Vienna, December 11th 1791

> Konstantia Mozart, née
> Weber, widow of the late
> Wolfgang Amadeus Mozart,
> Imperial State Kammer-
> kompositor*

This letter, written, no doubt, with the aid of a solicitor, shows an appreciation of her husband's true worth as a composer, which, taken by itself, is creditable. But we must also consider her resolute refusal to say anything about Mozart's anonymous dumping in an out-of-town graveyard and about the hideous Hofdemel tragedy, an eloquent silence which she maintained for the rest of her long life. After all, it was Constanze who destroyed Leopold Mozart's letters to his son written during the last years of his life, from January 12th 1781 to his death in 1788. There may well have been letters from

* Otto Deutsch, *Mozart: A Documentary Biography*, pp. 421, 422.

others, even including letters from Mozart himself, that she burnt at the same time.

While Constanze said nothing and did nothing to put matters right at the cemetery, the Church remained equally impassive. The bodies of men and women flung into these pits were usually left undisturbed for only seven years, but, since they were all nameless, no-one was expected to object if the priests in charge of the cemetery filled in the pits or removed the bones before that time. In the *Vaterländische Blätter*, of August 23rd 1808, an anonymous article about Mozart's burial revealed that Mozart's burial pit had been dug up and that 'those remains coming to the surface were not piled up, but ploughed back into the soil'.

Constanze must have known about these pits and the subsequent treatment of their contents. If she did not know about them when her husband was buried, she could easily have learnt the facts. Her lack of concern seems total, unlike that of Albrechtsberger, Mozart's successor as organist at St Stephen's. He went to the cemetery on the day after the funeral. Finding no mark whatsoever over the spot where Mozart lay, he may well have added his entreaties to those of Deiner's, that Constanze should take the trouble to carry out this simple task.

Eight years of silence had to elapse in the Austrian and German press before any comments were published about Mozart's ignominious burial. In 1799 the *Neuer Deutscher Merkur* reported that an Englishman, whose name was not given, had complained that 'the place in the cemetery, where Mozart's mortal frame (extinguished, perhaps, by violence) lies buried, remains unknown'. He contrasted this shameful act with the burial of Handel in Westminster Abbey forty years earlier. This, wrote the editor of the paper, 'is a hurtful reproach. Might there not be some reason for it?'

Meanwhile Constanze benefitted from the sale and performances of Mozart's music. In the year following his death, his admirer, the King of Prussia, Frederick William II, sent her the sum of 800 ducats, that is 3,600 gulden, for eight of his manuscripts, including an oratorio and two litanies. Following this great, but belated, kindness, the monarch then invited Constanze to Berlin to take part in a benefit concert on February 28th 1796. The first half consisted of the overture and two arias from *The Magic Flute*; in the second half, part of *La Clemenza di Tito* was sung by Constanze and five other singers. Mozart concerts were also given during these years in Vienna, Prague, Leipzig and Dresden; and Mozart's good friend, Michael Puchberg, continued to show his generosity by looking after Constanze's two children for a time after Mozart's death.

Just as Constanze did nothing to dispel the now open secret of Mozart's affair with Magdalena, the Freemasons, by their official reaction at his death, gave added credence to it. When such an inspired member completed his life on earth, a lengthy and eulogistic obituary would have been expected. But for Mozart there was just a brief summary of his life and work by Karl Hensler, the theatre director, in the bulletin of his Lodge.* On the banners of the Masons are proclaimed their active concern for the poor, especially for the poor who were members. But the death, the attempted murder and the suicide, which occurred on December 5th and 6th 1791, caused the most acute dilemma. Mozart and Hofdemel were friends and members of the same Lodge; the latter had tried to kill his wife and had committed suicide because of her conduct. If Hofdemel had killed his wife as well as himself, driven by guilt as well as jealousy, as the murderer of Mozart, then, obviously, she would never be able to tell anyone of his crime. If Mozart had been poisoned, the Masons may well have known this, and it would make them all the more taciturn about the whole appalling tragedy.

The reticence of the Masons at this time is indeed significant. Mozart was – and still is – their greatest musical genius. Although Maria Theresa, the Empress, was a staunch Catholic, her husband, Franz Stefan, joined the Masons, and

---

* Deutsch, *Mozart: A Documentary Biography*, p. 448, paras. 2 and 3. The rest of the oration is of a general nature.

many well educated men followed his example. Her son Joseph II, while not a member, looked on them with some sympathy, as he, like them, regarded himself as an enlightened reformist. Haydn became a Mason, as did Puchberg, Anton Stadler and Schikaneder. Any idea that the Masons were angry with Mozart, because he had divulged some of their secrets in *The Magic Flute*, is patently absurd. If this were true, they would no longer be secret. The opera reveals masonic symbols and tenets, but these ideas, of love, brotherhood and the need for courage and tenacity, are to be encouraged and disseminated around the world, not hidden in secrecy, and this is exactly what Mozart's great opera does. The creation of the opera was undoubtedly courageous, as many people, including Joseph's successor, Leopold II, held that Freemasonry and Christianity were incompatible. Twice in the eighteenth century, in 1738 and 1751, the Vatican had issued condemnations of this growing movement, in the Papal bulls of Clement XII and Benedict XIV. The Vatican today is still opposed to the brotherhood and its belief that all creeds are tentative and that none of them are absolutely true. Had it not been for Magdalena, there would have been nothing to stop the Freemasons expressing unstintedly their grief at Mozart's death and their admiration of his music.

In January 1792 Haydn wrote from London to Michael Puchberg, who had helped Mozart with loans on many occasions:

> For some time I was beside myself about Mozart's death, and I could not believe that Providence would so soon claim the life of such an indispensable man. I only regret that before his death he could not convince the English, who walk in darkness in this respect, of his greatness – a subject about which I have been sermonizing to them every single day. You will be good enough, my kind friend, to send me a catalogue of those pieces which are not yet known here, and I shall make every possible effort to promote such works for the widow's benefit; I wrote to the poor woman three weeks ago, and I told her that when her favourite son reaches the necessary age, I shall give him

composition lessons to the very best of my ability, and at no cost, so that he can, to some extent, fill his father's position.*

Seven years after Wolfgang's death, Constanze's aunt, Genoveva Weber, died, on March 13th 1798. She had sung as Constanze in *The Abduction from the Seraglio* four years earlier at the Weimar Court Theatre, where Goethe was the director. She and her husband, Franz Anton, had come to Salzburg, after the folding of his opera company. Genoveva's body was lowered into the grave of Constanze's father-in-law, Leopold Mozart, in the graveyard of St Sebastian's church in Salzburg. The coffin still rests on that of Leopold, who disliked and looked down on Constanze's family. Genoveva's son, Carl Maria, was given lessons in composition by Haydn's brother, Michael, in Salzburg, and later achieved fame as the founder of the romantic school in opera.

When Constanze was seventeen, her mother had increased her income by taking lodgers, one of whom Constanze married. Now, a widow in her thirties, Frau Mozart took the same step as her mother, and made one room of her flat available for a paying guest. In 1799 she took in an official from the Danish Embassy, Georg Nikolaus Nissen. He was a bachelor of thirty-seven, two years older than Constanze. The newcomer was a great admirer of Mozart's music, and he must have been highly surprised to find that most of his works, over five hundred, still lay unpublished in the Mozart apartment. Constanze, it seems, was not aware of their worth. Not more than seventy of her husband's works had been published while he was alive.

Nissen saw at once what should be done. Acting as Constanze's business manager, he set about the task of writing to music publishers and selling these many masterpieces. Only some thirty of Nissen's letters to the publisher, Anton André, have been preserved. Constanze added her signature to these letters, so they have been presented as her letters in the col-

* *The Collected Correspondence of Joseph Haydn.* H. C. Robbins Landon, p. 125.

lected edition of the Mozart correspondence. These business letters, written between 1800 and 1826, show that Nissen was certainly enthusiastic and efficient, although sometimes petulant and verbose. He was not a musician himself, and he could not have carried out this work without the aid of the Abbé Maximilian Stadler, Mozart's friend and a skilled musician. It was he who classified and catalogued the whole collection.

While the Abbé and the Danish embassy official continued their labours, the press maintained a general silence on the unanswered questions raised by Mozart's anonymous funeral. But any hopes that Constanze had that this reticence would be preserved at least as long as she was alive were dashed when a member of another embassy called on her and brought up the painful subject. This official, Georg Griesinger, councillor at the Saxon legation, read out to her the article that had appeared nine years before in the *Deutscher Merkur*, to refresh her memory. In the course of their discussion Constanze told him that she still had not visited the cemetery of St Marx. Somehow Griesinger persuaded her to do just this. He took her, Nissen and her son, Franz Xaver Wolfgang, now aged seventeen, to see the field where, officially, Austria's greatest son, was interred. Seventeen years had come and gone since then.

Griesinger followed this visit with an article in the *Vaterländische Blätter* of August 23rd 1808. He preferred to omit his name. The Austrian government, Magdalena and Constanze herself were still refusing to say anything about Mozart's death; in fact the subject was still an official secret. During Griesinger's conversation with Constanze, she told him that she 'fell dangerously ill immediately after Mozart died'. The article contained this information: 'Mozart's remains were buried in the field of St Marx, but the exact spot, unfortunately, cannot be given. Mozart died on December 5th 1791, and the corpses were buried, according to the gravedigger's account, in the third and fourth rows, counting from the cross standing in the cemetery.'

No mention was made of any official reason for the choice

of an unmarked, communal burial pit as Mozart's final resting place. The only explanation given in this short article was that 'Baron Swieten took care of Mozart's burial. He was only concerned to make the greatest possible saving for the bereaved family and the coffin was therefore lowered into a communal grave, and even the expense of a stone, which the widow would have liked to place there, had to be avoided.' It is hard to imagine that any reader failed to detect the fallaciousness of this story. What it implied was that the baron, a rich man, who could easily afford the cost of a decent burial, could not be bothered with such details.

Griesinger later wrote to the Viennese writer, Franz Gräffner, telling him that he had written this report about Constanze's visit to the cemetery:

> Arriving at God's field, we found that the gravedigger, during that year 1791, had been dead for a long time. The graves had since then been dug up, and any remains appearing on the surface had been ploughed back into the earth. There was nothing we could do, but enquire which rows had been used for burial in 1791. The gravedigger was only able to tell us that it was the third and fourth, coming down from the monumental cross, which stood in the middle of the field.

Griesinger's enquiries about the previous gravediggers proved fruitless. The one that he questioned was Josef Rothmayer. He had been working at the cemetery since 1802. The previous man was Simon Preischl, but he was only there for two years. His predecessor was dead, and no name could be discovered.

In 1809, after serving for ten years in Vienna, Georg Nissen was told that he would soon be recalled to Copenhagen. Constanze may well have feared that this good friend, like Süssmayr, would also vanish from her life, but this time there was no disappointment. Having shared the same address for the past decade, Constanze and Georg sealed their friendship by marriage at the cathedral in Pressburg (now Bratislava); they had unofficially been regarded as man and wife for some time. Napoleon had besieged Vienna in 1805 and was now inflicting another siege on the city in 1809, forcing many diplomats to leave. The Nissens lived in Pressburg, thirty miles east of Vienna, from the spring of 1808 until August 1809. Nissen had proved himself a good stepfather to the two children, Karl, now twenty-five, and Franz, eighteen. Constanze preferred to use Franz's third name, Wolfgang, as his first name perhaps reminded her of Süssmayr. Karl, who entered the civil service, was a good pianist and occasionally conducted at orchestral concerts. He worked in a subordinate post in Milan, then part of the Austrian Empire, and later, with the profits made by performances of *The Marriage of Figaro* in Paris, he retired and bought himself a country estate near Lake Como. He died, unmarried, at the age of seventy-five in 1859. His younger brother, who studied composition with Salieri and Albrechtsberger, became a music master and taught in Lvov, in Poland, part of the Austrian Empire. He died, also unmarried, in Carlsbad in 1844, aged fifty-five.

With no children to look after, Constanze was now free to leave the country with her new husband. In September 1810, they arrived in Copenhagen, where Nissen worked in the political censorship department for the next ten years. The Napoleonic War still had another five years to run before Denmark and the rest of the continent of Europe regained their independence. Nine years previously, Sir Hyde Parker, with Nelson second-in-command, had destroyed the Danish fleet off Copenhagen, as Denmark, Russia, Prussia and Sweden, as allies of France, had formed the Northern League to assist Napoleon by resisting the English navy's attempts to search vessels. Parker's victory and the assassination of Paul, the Russian Emperor, who admired Napoleon, broke up the Northern League.

After ten years' government service in Copenhagen, Nissen retired, and he and Constanze returned to Austria, choosing Salzburg as their last home. He now set to work on a biography of Mozart, which was almost complete when he died on March 22nd 1826, aged sixty-five. It was the first full-length study of the composer, but in it there are many omissions and misrepresentations. Not a word was included which sheds any light on the death, funeral or burial of Mozart; and no mention was made of Magdalena Hofdemel or of the suicide of her husband. However, Nissen does state that Mozart told his wife that he thought he had been poisoned; the only additional fact divulged on this subject is that Constanze tried to convince him that he was mistaken. There is, not surprisingly, no suggestion that Constanze was financially incompetent or extravagant; but here Nissen cannot be blamed, since no other biographer has found any evidence for such criticism. Room was made in Leopold Mozart's grave for Nissen's coffin. It was lowered into it, to join Constanze's father-in-law and her aunt Genoveva. Not content with this reverent disposal of her second husband, she piously erected over it an elaborate monument, consisting of an obelisk surrounded by four sets of stone flowers. Nissen's name is inscribed upon it, but not that of Leopold Mozart, her aunt or one of Nannerl's two children, who was also buried there. Nannerl had never liked Constanze, who had not bothered to let her know of her second marriage.

Constanze, widowed again, remained in Salzburg. After the death of Jakob Haibl, her sister, Sophie, came to Salzburg to live with her. Another sister, Aloysia, and Mozart's sister, Nannerl, also widowed, spent their last years in Salzburg. Constanze outlived two of her sisters, Josefa dying in 1819, Aloysia in 1839, and Nannerl, who died in 1830. The last Weber sister alive was Sophie, who died in 1843.

In 1915 a diary, written by Constanze, was found, which covered the years from 1824 to 1837. Sadly it is without a single interesting remark, made up entirely of mundane, insignificant details relating to household chores, meals, washing and the state of her health – an ordinary diary, in fact. There is no personal comment on Mozart. From time to time her sons came to stay with her. Apart from this we learn nothing of any interest.[*]

* Mozarteums-Mitteilungen 2 (1920), vol. 2 (38–62), vol. 3 (65–75).

When Constanze was sixty-six, in 1829, she was visited by two admirers of Mozart from England, Vincent Novello, the music publisher, composer and pianist, and his wife, Mary. The Novellos fully appreciated the genius of Mozart, Vincent with justification calling him the Shakespeare of music. Vincent and Mary both wrote a diary in which they described their continental tour, and this was only discovered in 1945 by their great-granddaughter in the family home in Fermo, in Italy, of the Gigliucci, into which family the Novellos' daughter, Clara, had married. When Vincent and Mary made this Mozart pilgrimage, they had no idea that Mozart's relationship with his wife might not have been perfect, and they knew nothing about his love of Magdalena. They did not therefore ask any questions which might have elicited further information on these subjects. Nevertheless some of Constanze's replies and some of the Novellos' reactions – and some of the remarks made by people who knew Mozart – clearly indicate that Constanze, for some reason, was not as devoted to Mozart as casual observers might think.

The number of negative statements recorded by the Novellos in their comments on their conversations with Constanze is in itself significant, especially when their respect and veneration towards the maestro's widow is taken into account. 'Description of Madame Nissen. Her face does not resemble the portrait given of her in [Nissen's] biography ... The way in which she spoke of her illustrious Husband was not quite so enthusiastic as I should have expected in one "so near and dear" to him.' [Vincent Novello]

Hoping to gain information from both Constanze and Nannerl, Mozart's sister, for a biography of the composer, Vincent Novello drafted two sets of questions. Nannerl, Madame von Sonnenburg, was too infirm to write, and Constanze was not prepared to comply on paper, but we do have her verbal answers.

Constanze's younger son, Franz Xaver, was visiting Salzburg at the time. She told the Novellos that she 'regretted that her son is so lazy a character. His father, she says, was so full of

energy and vivacity.' Mary Novello asked Constanze if she
had ever thought of writing an autobiography, or a sketch
about her life with Mozart and Nissen. 'No, she said, it was
too fatiguing to write about herself.' She then told them the
story about Mozart having an infectious disease, which she
hoped she would catch by throwing herself on his death-
bed, an incident which neither Sophie nor anyone else
mentioned.

When Mary Novello first met Constanze, she was 'so overcome with various emotions that I could do nothing but weep
and embrace her. She seemed also affected and said repeatedly
in French *"oh quelle bonheur pour moi, de voir les enthousiastes pour
mon Mozart"*. She speaks French fluently though with a
German accent. She is charmingly lodged in the Nun's street,
half way up a cliff from which a most extensive and charming
view is gained scarcely to be equalled in the world.' The
Novellos visited the third-floor apartment where Mozart was
born and they called on Nannerl, now 'blind, languid, feeble
and nearly speechless'. It must have surprised the English
couple when, on another visit to Constanze, she declared that
'there were moments when she not only prayed sincerely to
die but that she did not love her children; everything was
hateful to her in the world.'

Mary Novello asked her about Georg Nissen. 'She said he
was as amiable in his character as Mozart, that she could not
say which had been most kind to her, she could have wished to
live for both. Nissen's biography was undertaken with a view
to make a small sum for the two sons, but unfortunately it has
not yet paid its expenses.' Constanze then told the Novellos
that the Emperor, Joseph II, wondered why Mozart had not
married a rich wife. 'He said he hoped he should be able always
to gain sufficient by his genius to maintain the woman he
loved.' One afternoon they took a stroll with Franz Xaver.
'Walked arm in arm with him and afterward had the same
pleasure of having Mozart's widow as a companion in a stroll.
She walked between Mary and myself having hold of an arm
of each. He spoke very affectionately of his mother and of Mr.

Nissen, who brought him up like his own son and to whom he said he owed everything.'

The Novellos went to Mass in the cathedral in Salzburg, but they were 'disappointed at not having heard a single piece of Mozart's compositions' here or at any other church in the town. They found that St Peter's church, 'where Michael Haydn is buried, has some good paintings, and his monument is worth seeing. The burial ground is very picturesque.' Vincent Novello copied the Latin inscription on the momument, and noted that the names of twenty pieces of his sacred music were inscribed on it. This composer suffered no indignity at his death.

On the same day Constanze took her visitors to see the grave of her second husband and the monument which she had put up in his honour. They made no comment in their diary, except that 'it is a simple pyramid, with four inscriptions, and as usual surrounded by flowers.' The very next subject mentioned by Mary Novello is Copenhagen, and the enjoyable time spent there by Constanze and Nissen. 'Madame speaks with great pleasure of the society of Copenhagen, and of the time she spent there, although she was there twice while the English attacked that city.'

This was hardly true. England had attacked Copenhagen twice but this was before the Nissens came to Denmark. Parker and Nelson attacked the Danish fleet off Copenhagen in 1801, and a force of 30,000 men landed just north of the capital in 1807. On this occasion the central districts of the city were destroyed by a naval bombardment which went on for three nights; some 2,000 Danes were killed. For six weeks the town was occupied by the English and when they left they took away the bulk of the Danish fleet and two million pounds worth of naval stores.

Two embarrassing moments occurred when the Novellos were presented with personal possessions of Constanze. She showed Vincent a watch 'which had been made a present to him [Mozart] at Paris, and which he had given to her as a bridal present. It is a small gold one, going remarkably well. Though she had several presented to her since, she has never worn any but that one. She had it at that very time in her bosom.' Constanze then asked Vincent '*voulez-vous l'avoir?*' He tact-fully assumed that she was not being serious and declined it. She tried again:

> She also showed me the inkstand out of which he had written most of his works, amongst others the *Figaro, Don Giovanni,* the *Tito, Magic Flute* – and the Requiem. She has had the good taste to preserve it just in the same state as he left it, with all the blots running from the time he wrote the last page just before he died. This interesting relic consists of a little dark marble slab of an oblong shape, upon which is placed the silver metal vessel for the ink. On the opposite side is a vessel of the same shape, containing sand, and between the two is a little silver bell forming a cover for the wafers. As I evidently admired this relic, which is like the fountain whence had issued such exquis-itely beautiful creations, Madame was so kind as to ask me whether she should give it to me.
>
> The offer was so tempting a one that I rather hesitated in saying that I should be sorry to deprive her of what she valued so much. Had she repeated the offer, I own I would not then have been able to resist accepting what would have been such an invaluable treasure to me.

It was on the last day of their stay in Salzburg that Constanze told the Novellos that Mozart considered that he had been poisoned. 'July 17. Some six months before his death he was possessed with the idea of his being poisoned. "I know I must die", he exclaimed, "someone has given me aqua toffana."' [Mary Novello]

Constanze added to this startling information details about the composition of the Requiem, and suggested that he was not in his right mind, harbouring the illusion that he was writing this work for his own death. There is no evidence that in the summer of 1791 Mozart was feeling ill or depressed, either in his own letters or in the observations of those who knew him well. Both his letters and his compositions at that time suggest renewed confidence and optimism. After this fabrication, Constanze then added the inaccurate information that Mozart was given the post of *Kapellmeister* at St Stephen's cathedral only three days before his death, instead of saying that it was only the reversion of this post that was offered and that was made nine months earlier, in April of that year. She was admittedly an old woman of sixty-six and her memory may well have been fading. But, although Mozart had died thirty-eight years earlier, she professed to remember exactly what he said when he was given this post on his death-bed. According to her, he declared that at last he could please himself in his writing, and at last 'he could do something worthy.' Ever since Mozart quit the Archbishop of Salzburg's service, he had pleased himself and written what he wanted to write, and all his life he had composed works which were of the highest worth.

Although Mozart himself had made it clear that he was entrusting Süssmayr with the completion of the Requiem, Constanze, as already described, chose to give the task to Josef Eybler. Constanze must have given a somewhat confusing explanation of this surprising defiance of her husband's wishes to the Novellos, and in doing so she gave vent, briefly, to her feelings about the young man, still smouldering after all these years. 'Süssmayr', wrote Mary Novello, 'afterwards wrote to Breitkopf of Leipzig [the publisher] that he had written the principal part of this Requiem.' Then Constanze remarked that 'anyone could have written what he had done.'

After these visits the Novellos left Salzburg and travelled to Vienna. 'The three days I have passed at Salzburg,' wrote Vincent, 'with the widow and son of Mozart have been some of the most interesting, satisfying and gratifying that I have ever enjoyed.' Constanze herself made a brief comment on the English couple in her matter-of-fact diary: 'July 17 1829. Sent reply to Stumpff by Novello, very attractive man and altogether charming wife. These good people left today, July 17.'

She may well have been relieved when the questioning came to an end.

In Vienna the Novellos continued their musical pilgrimage. They had a two-hour conversation with Aloysia, Constanze's sister, during which, with hindsight, she was able to infer that she might have been happier married to Mozart than her sister was.

She [Aloysia] seems a very pleasant woman but broken by misfortune – she is parted from her husband who allows her so little that she is obliged to give lessons which at her age she finds a great hardship. She complains bitterly against the Viennese for their neglect of the family of Mozart and says he was frequently in the last extreme of poverty and died miserably poor, that they cannot even find the precise spot on which he was buried. She told me that Mozart always loved her until the day of his death, which to speak candidly she fears has occasioned a slight jealousy on the part of her sister. I asked her why she refused him; she could not tell; the fathers were both agreed but she could not love him at the time. She was not capable of appreciating his talent and his amiable character, but afterwards she much regretted it. She spoke of him with great tenderness and regret.   [Mary Novello]

After hearing Aloysia's disturbing comments about Mozart's unmarked grave, the Novellos may have been surprised to find further indications that the Viennese did not share their optimistic assumption that all aspects of the Mozart household were a matter of sweetness and light.

Mr. Streicher to dinner, one of the most eminent Pianoforte makers in Vienna. He was acquainted with Mozart during the last part of his career and gave Mozart's younger son his first lessons on the Piano Forte. Mr. Streicher's opinions of the widow are not so favourable as what I could have wished; but as he said very little upon the subject, which seemed to be a sore one, I of course do not feel authorised to repeat a single word of what passed. Truth I shall always endeavour to ascertain upon every occasion and shall record faithfully for the gratification of those who [word omitted] upon subjects which concern the public; but private affairs and gossip upon matters with which the world at large has nothing to do I have not the least inclination either to learn or to record. [Vincent Novello]

What caused Novello to write such a laboured excuse for refusing to divulge what he had been told on this occasion is left for the reader to imagine.

Dined today with Mr. Streicher who knew Mozart. He was very severe upon Mme. Mozart and afraid if he told Vin any anecdotes respecting her husband that his name should appear for fear of hurting her feelings. [Mary Novello]

Judging by the odd wording of this sentence, the only muddled, badly written passage in her diary, Mrs. Novello was similarly affected by Streicher's disclosures. She then went on to reveal that, during a further conversation, 'Mr. Streicher was very chatty – he says it was Madame's fault that no monument is erected to Mozart but does not quite prove why.'

He was evidently unable to give the Novellos the whole story. Vincent Novello remarked that 'Mozart's monument is a sore subject with Streicher and every other person of good taste and feeling I have yet met with.' Whether he was conscious of it or not, Novello was here delivering, by implication, a justified condemnation of Constanze.

Criticism of Mozart himself came from two other friends of the composer with whom the Novellos dined, Abbé Maximilian Stadler and the banker, Joseph Henickstein. Mozart, the Novellos were told, 'would not take pains in giving lessons to any ladies but those he was in love with . . . He was always in love with his pupils.' On the following day the chambermaid at the inn where the English couple were staying commented on the private life of the Viennese, making the Novellos perhaps, after these allusions, think of Mozart and Constanze. 'In Vienna', she said, 'the husband sleeps in one end of the house and the wife at the other. The husband cares for every woman better than his own wife, and she repays the compliment.'

In their efforts to find out more about Mozart's burial, the Novellos found themselves up against a brick wall of silence. They met Tobias Haslinger, the music publisher and friend of Beethoven, and Josef Eybler, whom Constanze had asked to complete the unfinished Requiem. Although he had been unable to finish it, he did not give the score back to Constanze; he still had a copy when the Novellos met him. Having talked about the Requiem, without discovering which sections had been composed by him and which were the work of Süssmayr, Vincent Novello bluntly asked this question: 'Where is Mozart's monument?'

All Eybler and Haslinger could reply was 'Where indeed?' The Novellos could not see any monument erected in honour of Mozart, but they were able to see the house in the centre of the town in which he had a comfortable seven-room apartment.

> It is a handsome looking house with five windows in front. It was not without strange sensations that I ascended the identical stairs which he had so often passed, and down which he was at last brought down as a corpse. But as the family could not be disturbed, I was prevented from obtaining access to the apartment where he expired when the pen dropped from his hand. [Vincent Novello]

The visitors noticed a painting and a sculpture on the house which have some bearing on Mozart's own divided allegiance.

> Curious that over Mozart's house in Vienna there is a painting of the Virgin and Child and under the painting there is a very tasteful ornament in sculpture of Venus with the world under her feet, surrounded by very graceful folds of drapery and clouds above of an elegant form. [Vincent Novello]

On July 25th 1829 Vincent Novello walked to the church of St Marx, on the outskirts of the capital, to see for himself the place where Mozart had been buried.

The church, or rather chapel, is a very small one, with only one altar and no side aisles, three windows on each side and no galleries. The only part of the very confined space surrounding the church is on the left-hand side of the church where there are a few grave stones stuck up against the surrounding walls; the whole cannot be above fifty feet square, if so much. You may be sure I walked over every part of it with the utmost veneration and in every path; but there was not only no stone to be found with his name upon it, but there were scarcely any traces to be found of a single grave. The reports I had heard were but too true. I returned completely disgusted with the tasteless apathy, the heartless ingratitude and disgraceful neglect with which this great man was treated by the generality of his countrymen and by the Viennese in particular.

Constanze was still alive eleven years later when the fiftieth anniversary of Mozart's death approached with the St Marx graveyard still destitute of any memorial. Incensed by this continued paralysis, Ritter Johann von Lucam, a member of the Society of Friends of Music, wrote to Constanze, asking her to cast her mind back to 1791 and tell him something about her husband's funeral. She took the trouble to reply, on October 14th 1841. She gave, as the main reason for her inability to answer some of the questions, her extreme grief at Mozart's death and an unspecified illness which she had then contracted. She stated that she was prevented from accompanying her husband's coffin to the cemetery by the extremely harsh wintry weather. In the course of time, she assured him, she did indeed visit the grave of her 'unforgettable husband'.

Alas, all effort was in vain. The gravedigger told me that his predecessor had died recently. He therefore could not know who was buried there before he had started work there. I and my friends searched the entire cemetery with no success at all, since there could not be found the slightest clue.

It was the custom then for the departed to be collected only by the hearse, driven to the consecration in the church and then taken without further ado to the grave; it unfortunately happened that none of Mozart's friends went with the corpse, making it thereby impossible to gain information from anyone as to the place of the burial. One will be indulgent considering my great pain and my youth, in that during the misfortune which shattered my entire being and numbed my senses, I did not think of having the place of the grave marked. A misfortune, of which one has so many to regret in life. I was also reassured by the custom, usual in Catholic countries, of marking the burial place with a cross, bearing the name of the departed, but which also unfortunately was overlooked.

At any event, I know for certain that my husband was buried at St Marx cemetery. Although unfortunate events have made it impossible to raise his remains with any confidence, I feel strongly about this intention, which particularly honours the departed man. Therefore it only remains for the citizens of Vienna, who wish to glorify his memory, to erect a memorial to him in this cemetery – a somewhat unsatisfactory solution. It was always my personal and most deeply felt wish to order a worthy memorial to him to be built at the cemetery where he lies buried, and perhaps this wish will now be realised, which certainly will be a great joy to me.*

Nine years previously in 1832, Constanze had received another visitor, Ludwig I, King of Bavaria, who gave her an additional pension. He too asked her about her failure to mark the grave, and she gave the feeble excuse she repeated to von Lucam, that the local priests should have carried out this particular task.

On March 6th 1842 Constanze died, aged seventy-nine, and her body was deposited in the grave of her father-in-law, Leopold Mozart, alongside that of her second husband, Georg Nissen. She and her sisters all died without once revealing a word about the death of Mozart, his burial or his beloved Magdalena. She also remained silent.

* Hermine Cloeter, *Die Grabstätte Mozarts* (Vienna, 1956), p. 66.

Epilogue

THE SUBSEQUENT HISTORY of Vienna's official recognition of Austria's greatest son speaks volumes in its embarrassment, its procrastination and its still existing fear of divulging the full story of Mozart's death and burial.

In a second letter to von Lucam, in 1841, Constanze told him that Karl Scholl, now an old man, who had been a flautist at the Hofoper, might be able to tell him where Mozart was buried – if he was still alive. The flautist was still among the living, but was too infirm to make the journey to the cemetery. Lucam visited the homes of two other musicians who said they knew where he lay, but they too would not, or could not, go with him to the graveyard. Scholl told Lucam that Mozart was buried near Albrechtsberger's grave. As the year 1856, the centenary of Mozart's birth, approached, the Mayor of Vienna, Ritter von Seillern set up a committee to discuss both the mysterious death of the composer and the question of a memorial. In November 1855 this committee invited Albrechtsberger's grandson, an accountant, Karl Friedrich Hirsch, to tell them what he could about the burial. As a child he could remember visiting his grandfather's grave; he also claimed to know where Mozart, together with some unknown people, had been buried. The gravedigger at St Marx was then instructed to prepare a place at the St Marx cemetery for a monument to be placed on what now was taken to be the hallowed spot. A sculptor, Hans Gasser, was chosen to create a fitting memorial.

It was now discovered that a willow shrub was growing on the spot chosen for the monument. A former gravedigger, Radschopf, was questioned about this, and he disclosed that it had been planted there by an admirer of Mozart, a master tailor. Like the maestro, this benefactor remained anonymous. This planting was against the rules and regulations, but as officialdom had failed to mark the burial place, an ordinary member of the public had come forward and had taken the law into his own hands. The anniversary year came and went and still the cemetery remained without a monument.

At last, in 1859, sixty-eight years late, Hans Gasser's statue of a grieving muse, in bronze, arrived at the cemetery and was at last erected, not where the willow shrub marked the spot, supposedly, but a little way off. Doubts and confusion still reigned. One might have thought that this was the end of the story, but only nine years later this monument, lying unguarded in the suburban graveyard, was vandalised; parts of the statue were broken off. In the following decade the bronze medallion of Mozart's head disappeared. It was suggested that Gasser should be asked to reconstitute the memorial but he was now dead. In 1891, the centenary of Mozart's death, this embarrassing matter was once more discussed officially. After duly debating the question, the Mayor and his advisers made a decision. The monument was removed to the capital's Central Cemetery, where Mozart was certainly not buried. The cemetery at St Marx church returned to its former state.

Once again the public took the law into its own hands. Another admirer of Mozart, once again anonymously, deposited a large stone slab in the middle of the cemetery; on it was the name of Mozart, the date of his birth and death, not engraved but painted, roughly, in black. Only towards the end of the century was something done to erect a fitting memorial in the graveyard. Alexander Kugler, who later became the official guardian of the place, removed the inappropriate slab, and, unofficially, assembled his own memorial. He placed a statue of a weeping angel on the supposed site of the communal burial pit, added a stone tablet with the name and relevant dates upon it, and a broken pillar stump – parts of other people's gravestones.

This unofficial memorial stands there today in the middle of this cemetery, which now contains six thousand graves. Franz Niemeczek, Mozart's first biographer, Anna Gottlieb, *The Magic Flute*'s first Pamina, and Johann Albrechtsberger all lie there. Two small signs help the visitor to find his way to Mozart's supposed grave.

Bibliography

The Letters of Mozart and His Family, trans. Emily Anderson, 1938. Second edition, 1966 (Macmillan)

Otto Erich Deutsch, *Mozart: A Documentary Biography*, trans. Eric Blom, Peter Branscombe and Jeremy Noble, 1965 (A. & C. Black)

Ivor Keys, *Mozart, His Music in his Life*, 1980 (Granada)

Michael Levey, *The Life and Death of Mozart*, 1971 (Weidenfeld)

Vincent and Mary Novello, *A Mozart Pilgrimage*, ed. Rosemary Hughes, 1955 (Novello)

Sacheverell Sitwell, *Mozart*, 1933 (Peter Davies)

Arthur Hutchings, *Mozart, the Man, the Music*, 1976 (OUP)

Hugh Ottoway, *Mozart*, 1979 (Thames & Hudson)

W. J. Turner, *Mozart*, 1938 (Gollancz), 1965 (Methuen)

Alfred Einstein, *Mozart*, 1946 (Cassell)

Carl Bär, *Mozart: Krankheit, Tod, Begräbnis*, 1966 (Salzburg)

Friedrich Kerst, *Mozart, in his own Words*, 1965 (Dover)

Robert Pack and Marjorie Lelash, *Mozart's Librettos*, 1961 (Meridian)

Brigid Brophy, *Mozart, the Dramatist*, 1974 (Faber)

Mozart's Apartment, Museums of Vienna (1921)

Hermine Cloeter, *Die Grabstätte Mozarts*, 1956 (Vienna)

A. Schurig, *Konstanze Mozart*, 1922 (Dresden)

G. Leopold Schefer, *Mozart und Seine Freundin*, in *Orpheus, Musikalisches Album*, 1841 (Vienna)

Ernst Weizmann, *Der Unbekannte Mozart*, 1956. Die Weltpresse, Vienna. 4.2.56–28.4.56

O. E. Deutsch, *Die Legende von Mozarts Vergiftung*, Mozart-Jahrbuch, 1964 (Salzburg)

Dieter Schickling, *Einige ungeklärte Fragen zur Geschichte der Requiem-Vollendung*, Mozart-Jahrbuch, 1976/77 (Salzburg)

Joseph Eibl, *Süssmayr und Constanze*, Mozart-Jahrbuch (Salzburg) 1976/7

Ludwig Paneth, *Constanze – Eine Ehrenrettung*, Mozart-Jahrbuch, 1959 (Salzburg)

C. M. Girdlestone, *Mozart's Piano Concertos*, 1948 (Cassell)

Arthur Hutchings, *Companion to Mozart's Piano Concertos*, 1948 (OUP)

Saul K. Padover, Joseph II, *The Revolutionary Emperor* (Eyre & Spottiswoode, 1967)

J. Frank Bright, *Joseph II* (Macmillan, 1897)

Robert A. Kann, *A History of the Habsburg Empire*, *1526–1918* (University of California Press, 1974)

Paul P. Bernard, *Joseph II and Bavaria*, Martinus Nijhoff, 1965)

The author is very grateful to Professor Otto Schneider of the Mozart Institute, Vienna, and Dr Rudolph Angermüller of the Mozarteum, Salzburg for their assistance and to Angi Rutter, Christine Stone and Hannelore Schmidt for their help in translation.

Index